ANGLICANS IN BRITTANY

Anglicans in Brittany

The Story of St Bartholomew's, Dinard

Revd Alan C. Charters

SERENDIPITY

Copyright © Revd Alan C. Charters, 2003

First published in 2003 by
Serendipity
Suite 530
37 Store Street
Bloomsbury
London

British Library Cataloguing-in-Publication data
A record for this book is available from the British Library

ISBN 1 84394 044 2

Printed and bound by Bookcraft Ltd, Bath

Dedicated to Audrey and Julian Thompson

Contents

Foreword

by the Right Reverend Frank Sargeant,
Assistant Bishop in Europe,
formerly Bishop of Stockport and Bishop at Lambeth

One of the undoubted achievements of the Church of England during the nineteenth and twentieth centuries was its expansion from an exclusive national Church with an Erastian polity into a worldwide communion embracing people of every race and colour. Although this development was greatly assisted by Great Britain's colonial expansion, the progress of the Anglican Church was by no means limited to English-speaking areas. The growth of Anglican congregations in Europe is a striking tribute to the dedication of generations of Anglican worshippers who have introduced their particular forms of worship to their neighbours wherever they have settled.

In this new and carefully researched study of the foundation and growth of St Bartholomew's church, Dinard, Alan Charters captures the religious and social contribution which American, Canadian and English ex-patriots who have made their home in North Brittany have made to the local culture and amenities enjoyed by residents and visitors alike. These include the founding of the local tennis and golf clubs, the British/American church with its splendid library of English books and, more recently, the Lord Russell Association for the mutual appreciation and understanding of French and British cultural traditions.

Although St Barthlolomew's represented a *religion in-connue* in legal French terms, the church soon endeared itself to the local French and émigré population who now regard it as an integral part of the cultural life of the region. Local support has included financial aid in times of difficulty and relations with the local Roman Catholics and the Église Reformée have always been warm and friendly. The church remains stronger than ever to welcome new settlers and visitors from many nations who meet for worship every Sunday.

This is a story waiting to be written and I am grateful to my old friend Alan Charters for giving us the opportunity to consider the contribution which faithful Anglicans have made to the presentation of the Gospel and the social life of the Church in one of the most popular French resorts today.

✠   Frank P. Sargeant

Acknowledgements

I am most grateful to Julian Thompson and other members of the Council of St Barthlolomew's, Dinard, for permission to make full use of the minutes and archives of the church and many other documents discovered during the research. Without their constant help and encouragement this book would never have been completed.

It gives me great pleasure to acknowledge the kindly help of Catherine Wakeley of USPG, who put me on to the track of valuable sources of information held in the Rhodes Library at Oxford and to the staff of the library for their time and generosity in keeping me supplied with the X Files containing the records of the Continental Chaplains Committee and a wealth of other documentary information. To Adrian Mumford, Secretary of the Diocese in Europe, I owe thanks for his helpfulness in obtaining permission for me to gain access to currently closed material, held at the Guildhall Library under the thirty-year rule and which is not yet catalogued. In the realisation that I could only afford to spend a limited amount of time in London, Stephan Freeth, Keeper of Manuscripts, went out of his way to ensure that all the relevant material was promptly available and Sharon Duff showed an equal enthusiasm in digging out papers and manuscripts which she considered might be of interest to me.

In France the staff of the Museum in Dinard have been most helpful and encouraging, as were the staff of the municipal archives who also enabled me to discover material held in the archives of Rennes. In particular, Monsieur

Henri Fermin, former curator of the Museum, has been most helpful in offering old photographs from his remarkable collection. Special thanks are offered to the Université de Haute Bretagne, in particular for guiding me to the thesis by M. Jean Pierre Lambrouin under the supervision of Professor R. Leseine on 'The British in the Dinan–Dinard area, 1650–1992'.

I am delighted to dedicate this work to the ever-patient Frances, who may have expected to see more of me in the last two years but has had to put up with my regular absences and pre-occupation for longer than she deserves.

All the opinions and interpretations of the material in the text are entirely my own.

Alan C. Charters

Talgarth, September 2002

List of illustrations

CHAPTER ONE

The British Community in Brittany

Long before the Roman period, when sea travel was so much less hazardous than journeys on land, Brittany attracted immigrants from the islands which have become known as Great Britain. Archaeological deposits clearly demonstrate that there were regular trading and social contacts between the peoples on either side of the Channel. The Romans themselves probably recognised the kinship that already existed between the two regions when they were content to name them Britania and Britania Minor or Cismarius respectively. But the first major migration for which we have certain evidence is after the collapse of the Roman Empire when Welsh and Irish 'saints' of the Celtic persuasion crossed the sea to spread their faith and culture which was threatened by successive invasions from the pagan hordes which swept across England.

During the fifth and sixth centuries, Welsh Christianity in particular was enjoying a resurgence of missionary zeal fostered by the powerful intellectual learning of the Celtic monasteries under the leadership of men like Dubricius. In spite of pressure from the invading forces which was forcing them further back into the mountains of West Wales, they set out to spread the Good News and their learning amongst their sympathetic neighbours to the south. The monks who led the advance into Brittany took their native culture with them with the result that many church dedications in Brittany share the same Celtic names as those found in Wales and to this day there are striking affinities between the local language and dialects of both regions. Welsh speakers claim to be able to converse without difficulty with those who speak the Breton patois. St Samson, St Suliac, St Enogat and the others would soon have felt equally at home in Brittany as in their native Wales.

During the Middle Ages it is likely that immigration and colonisation were in the opposite direction for many of the followers of William the Conqueror and their successors had lands in Brittany. For some centuries Norman and Breton families owned land on both sides of the Channel and the bonds between the two regions were strengthened by inter-marriage until the growth of nationalism and the loss of the 'English' land in France created the divisions which have survived to modern times.

It is not until the mid and late seventeenth century that we find another significant migration from Ireland and parts of Cornwall to northern Brittany after the fierce campaigns of Oliver Cromwell and the later conquest by King William III which resulted in his victory at the Battle of the Boyne. Irish Roman Catholics fled to a land, perceived to be more sympathetic and tolerant to their cause and, by all accounts, they rapidly integrated with the local community, adopting Francophile names still recognisable today such as Ouançon (from Cunis O'Hamon), Cogrennes and Cograines. Many of these refugees settled in Dinan.

During the wars of the eighteenth century, Dinan was chosen as a billeting town for English prisoners of war. While there is evidence that the good people of the town welcomed the billeting of the prisoners on account of the allowances they earned from a grateful government, there are also records of the frustrations suffered by the town authorities, whose responsibility they became. Some of these prisoners, soldiers and sailors, persisted in escaping and causing much aggravation for their guards who had to

account for their disappearance. Yet it appears that conditions were no more harsh for the private soldier than if they
had remained in their cottages and hovels in the developing
industrial towns of Great Britain. In 1757 it was reported that
there were two thousand prisoners in a town of six thousand
French, and ninety guards had to be mounted daily to over-
see them. 'You met them (the prisoners) in the streets, the
cafes and making good friends of family households.' One
young naval officer, whose ship had blown ashore during
the American War, was detained in Dinan before becoming
one of the best known and loved clergymen and men of
letters of the nineteenth century, the Reverend Sidney Smith.

Although a number of prisoners in Dinan died of 'the
white plague', a form of typhoid, and were buried outside
the town walls in 'le clos des Anglais', the town also became
a favourite resort as a watering hole in times of peace where
the well-to-do English could drink the minerals at the 'Fon-
taine des Eaux' which, it was claimed, 'guerit les maladies'.
So popular was this that the Reverend Etienne Gilbert, an
Anglican clergyman based in Guernsey, received permission
from the Mayor to conduct religious services in Dinan for
the English. He is the first known Anglican priest to have
permission to minister amongst his fellow English speaking
comrades in Brittany, although the permission came from
the French civil authorities and not from the Bishop.

At the end of the Napoleonic Wars in 1815 some prisoners
preferred to remain in Dinan and some of the officers even
brought their wives and families to join them, believing
their prospects in rural Brittany to be better than in industrial Britain. They were joined by other Royal Navy officers
who had been placed on the reserve and who had to endure
half pay. Dinan was a convenient town for them for their
port of recall was Jersey and it was easier for them to keep
in touch with the Channel Islands from there than from the
English mainland. From the 1830s Dinan became popular

with ex-Indian Army officers who had enjoyed a busy but not altogether demanding life, but many suffered from tropical diseases. They found that their pensions stretched further in Dinan than in the expensively fashionable spa towns of Bath and Cheltenham. However those who did not integrate rapidly into the local population became bored with the ghetto-type existence of the small English-speaking community and were inclined to move on to Bordeaux, Switzerland or even German resorts like Wiesbaden. Many eventually returned to Britain.

Most British residents on the whole did not stay for more than five to ten years although one or two families, like John Surtees, bought mansions. The 1841 census revealed that there were only 129 permanent British residents. This was enough to encourage the Reverend Hugh Thomas Oxenham to hold Anglican services in La Lainerie from 1843 for there were many 'floating visitors' as well as a steady increase of more permanent migrants. By 1861 the British population had spread throughout Brittany and there were at least 1629 (759 men and 870 women) living in the Cote d'Armor. In 1867 the sous-Prefect of Dinan estimated that five per cent of the town's population was British. By 1870 the population of Dinan had peaked with some 502 British permanent residents, two thirds of whom were women, spinsters and widows looked after by nieces or domestics. The Mayor evaluated the economic benefit of the British to the local community as 1,500,000 Francs, thus showing that voluntary British incomers had more than maintained the benefits the townspeople had received from their role as guardians of prisoners of war.

The British colony in Dinan became the model for other colonies including its successor in Dinard. But it was a largely barren community which failed to produce offspring who would continue to live in Dinan. The young boys returned to England for education and did not return except for holidays. There is no record of a wedding being celebrated in the Anglican church after it was built and there was no one to maintain the English-speaking population in the future. At the outbreak of the First World War, there were only 42 British residents out of a total population of 11,410. Exceptionally Miss Bouton, who came to Dinan with her parents in 1828, was still living there with other elderly spinsters in the twentieth century.

One of the factors contributing to the decline of the British colony in Dinan was the discovery of Dinard, a small fishing village, by the more well-to-do. One of these was Mr William Faber of Darrington in Yorkshire, who came to live at Les Buttes in Dinan, possibly for health reasons, for he died in 1854 at the age of 42. He was not the first British resident of Dinard for the old Prieuré had become a favoured residence of Mr Sedgewick, British Consul at St Malo in 1830, who passed it on to his successor Mr Alwyn Thomson in 1840 who then transferred the house to Mr Robert Thomson Monteith in 1850.

The name Faber has become intimately connected with the church of St Bartholomew's which is now in rue Faber, for his widow, Mrs Lyona Faber, remained in Dinard, renting Les Buttes and investing in other building plots with her husband's legacy. She encouraged her friends to move to Dinard, amongst whom was James Erhart Coppinger and his wife, née Tudor-Hart, who, though born in London, had made a fortune in the United States and became an American citizen in 1858. He was the first of a strong contingent of American citizens to reside in Dinard and he built the 'Chateau du Bec de la Vallee', having first lived at Le Moulinet. Another wealthy American, Mr Carmac from Philadelphia and his wife Nadine Kalpascmikoff rented and then bought the Villa Rochedependante. Mrs Tudor-Hart's niece came to Dinard from Canada and other residents moved in from Avranches, Pau and the Channel Isles. In the meantime Mrs Faber built the 'Villa St Catherine' and others who purchased building plots from her built their own prosperous houses, mostly using contractors from Jersey. In due course Mrs Faber's daughter married Captain Hody Cox, a Devonshire gentleman, and Mrs Faber's son, another William, sold St Catherine's villa to Mrs Brydon, whose daughter married Reginald Forbes. All of these wealthy residents were to become key figures in the early years of the Anglican Church which itself became an important centre for the English-speaking community.

And so was born a tight circle of wealthy English-speaking friends who rapidly made Dinard a centre of elegance and gracious living, thus creating the most luxurious and pleasurable British society on the Continent of Europe. Many summer visitors were attracted including the Prince of Wales, later King Edward VII, the young Winston Churchill and the Duke and Duchess of Connaught. The arrival of the mysterious Joseph Rochaid, a Lebanese entrepreneur reminiscent of Anthony Trollope's Mr Mermotte of *The Way We Live Now* and his wife Marie Marthe Dadah encouraged the growth of the British colony still further. With large funds at his disposal, he bought several hundred sites very cheaply and during the next quarter of a century, prospered in business as a financial, property and real estate agent.

The expansion of Dinard was dramatic. The 1872 census counted 2,513 inhabitants of whom only four British American families were registered as permanent residents. Many of the property owners came only for the summer season from May to September but other visitors rose from over 500 in the 1870s to well over 2000 during the Edwardian period.

Apart from the mildness of the climate, the beauty of the area, the reported purity of the air and the advantages to the domestic economy, many prosperous visitors found it a welcome escape from the moral strictures of conventional

Victorian England and found they could enjoy the gaming tables of the Casino and the courtly flirtations of the regular round of Balls and soirées without unnecessary embarrassment. Dinard became the Brighton of the continent, benefiting from its easy access from the British Channel Islands and the southern channel ports of Great Britain.

Dinard continued to attract residents and visitors in large numbers until the Second World War, after which the general state of the economy and the regulations limiting the amount of money which British citizens were allowed to take abroad (£25 per passport) made overseas visits more difficult and the British population declined. However during the late 1980s and 1990s there has been a massive new migration of people, escaping from an overcrowded southern Britain to what is perceived as a better quality of life with traditional values. Ease of transport and communication and the growing awareness of the European Union, together with the introduction of the Euro may ensure that the numbers of British migrants will continue into the future. At the end of 2001 it was estimated that there are at least 35,000 British citizens resident in Brittany.

The Church's Role

Meanwhile, the Church of England was becoming aware that many of her flock had left the Island shores for other lands in the growing Empire and the continent of Europe. The Society for the Propagation of the Gospel in Foreign Parts found that its statutes included responsibility for providing spiritual care of English residents in Europe who were deprived of the comforts of their national Church, and an informal group of churchmen met to address this problem under the authority of the Bishop of London.

Brittany was soon to become an object of the society's intentions, for on 18th August 1865 a letter was received from an English inhabitant of Guingamp in Western Brittany which described the 'spiritually neglected and destitute conditions of numbers of British residents scattered through various parts of Brittany and the North West of France.' It went on to urgently recommend 'a chaplain to be stationed at Guingamp as a central position in respect of the district referred to.' The Committee was unsure about its role but wrote to the Reverend F. W. Watson who was already living in Dinan and conducting Anglican services on an unofficial basis. Although Mr Watson does not appear to have taken action on this issue, and it is difficult to see how he could have handled such a general request in the short term, he was sufficiently encouraged to hasten the building of the Anglican church in Dinan. One of the first gifts to the new church is a handsome pewter goblet 'presented to the Protestant church in Dinan by the Reverend F. W. Watson in 1861' which is now in the possession of St Bartholomew's, Dinard. This is the earliest piece of church plate belonging to the Anglican communion in Brittany.

Back in London, the Continental Chaplains Committee was formally sanctioned on 27th November 1862 under the chairmanship of the Dean of Westminster, the Very Reverend Richard C. French after extensive enquiries on the Continent about the spiritual requirements of British citizens living there. At the first meeting the committee set out its constitution with commendable clarity and firmness. Its purpose was 'to support chaplains where there are large numbers of British sailors, labourers or other British subjects of poor condition' and they took it upon themselves to communicate with universities, British consuls, chaplains abroad, hotel keepers and 'influential persons in places frequented by British subjects.' They also undertook to 'raise and administer a special fund' for the work which was considered to be so important and urgent that the Committee met weekly on a Thursday at noon.

An early decision of the Committee on 11th December 1862 was that they should 'send abroad only approved clergymen under the sanction of the Bishop of London and his suffragan.' Acting on behalf of the Church of England this SPG Committee, together with the Bishop of London, was anxious to establish a strict control of Anglican activities on the continent of Europe. As soon as its existence became known it was dealing with requests from all over the Continent and by 12th March 1863, the Committee was asking for volunteers to undertake visits and carry out Confirmation services. At least four diocesan bishops offered their services, including those of Tasmania and Montreal, but in the end the task was accomplished by the Bishop of Jamaica!

The creation of this central committee in London as part of the SPG contribution to the world-wide Anglican church was to have a profound significance for the Anglican presence in Europe and, as far as St Bartholomew's was concerned, began to create tensions about the authority and management of the church which are only now beginning to be resolved.

The problems were to some extent anticipated, for as early as 1864 there was a serious debate in the revitalised Church Convocation which led to the consideration of a suffragan Bishop of the Channel Islands who would reside in Dover and be responsible for confirmations and visitations in Europe. In the end, an alternative unsatisfactory solution was preferred whereby a variety of bishops from the developing world-wide Anglican Communion were appointed to travel Europe to conduct confirmations which they presumably combined with a pleasurable latter-day Grand Tour. In 1864, for example, the Bishops of Oxford, Edinburgh, Guiana and Victoria all visited Europe and this was the first year for which the SPG published a list of Anglican services available on the Continent.

CHAPTER TWO

The Houses Built on Sand

Christ Church, Dinan

Just as the central authorities of the Church of England were formulating their plans in London, Anglicans on the north coast of Brittany were eagerly pressing forward with requests. Of the British communities, the strongest in the mid-nineteenth century was that of Dinan. Most of the settlers were Anglicans, of whom the best known was Colonel Kitchener, father of the future First World War Field Marshal. As early as 1833 the French authorities had allowed the use of a room in the former Palais de Justice and the congregation was deemed to be an ecclesiastical 'parish' under the jurisdiction of the Bishop of London. In 1862 the Maire of Dinan urged the municipal council to give permission for the community to erect a special building but funds were lacking and the project was abandoned.

In 1866 three men, Mr Logal Downes, Mr Charles Barton and the Reverend William Watson, who had been given a licence to preach in 1861, bought a plot of land and wrote to SPG requesting aid to complete the building of the church, which would then 'be placed in connexion with the Society.' The Continental Churches Committee resolved on a grant of £10 along with a loan of £100 on condition that the patronage of the church should be vested in the Society.

It needs to be remembered that, at this time, most English parish churches were in the hands of private patrons, with whom lay the power of appointment. The bishop of the diocese had the power of veto if he considered the applicant to be unsuitable by refusing a licence to the priest concerned, but this was rarely done.

On 19th November 1866, the Reverend F. W. Watson was able to write to SPG with the news that he had received an anonymous donation of £500 towards the building of the church, whereupon the Committee doubled their grant to £20 and formally accepted the ownership and patronage. While the French authorities were supportive and helpful – and it was even reported that the anglophile Emperor Napoleon III was sympathetic – the church did not qualify for any grant from French sources as Anglican worship was a *religion inconnue* in French law.

The foundation stone was laid on 28th July 1868 in the presence of the sous-Prefect, the maire and representatives of the Church of England. The completion of the church was delayed through lack of funds and by the death of the chaplain in 1869 as well as the outbreak of the Franco-Prussian War, and it was not until Whitsunday 1877 that a Scottish bishop, delegated by the Bishop of London came to consecrate the building. By happy coincidence the festivities were enriched by the presence of the band of the 12th Hussars which was playing nearby.

The statutes approved by SPG were based on the rules of governance which applied in most English parishes. Two churchwardens were to be appointed, one by the chaplain, the other to be chosen by the congregation and four other laymen were to form a committee of management. This committee was to be responsible for the chaplain's stipend and all church expenses. One of the conditions imposed by the Roman Catholic bishop during the time of the Concordat of the Roman Church with the French State was that an Anglican church must exist solely for the purpose of ministering to British people abroad. No proselytising of any kind was permitted amongst the local population. It is therefore all the more surprising that one of the first church-wardens should be a Frenchman!

Cosme Antoine François de Satge was a nephew of Oscar de Satge, Baron of Thoren, who had rented a house in Dinan during the 1860s. This royalist family had been ruined by the Revolution and had sought refuge in England where Oscar's father had married Harriet Rowley, daughter of Lord Longford. Oscar also married an English girl, Millicent Wall, and, although the young Cosme was edu-cated in France at the University of Paris and in Toulouse to complete his studies as a barrister, he spent a great deal of time with his British relations in Ireland and London.

We are informed that the family was not exactly overjoyed when he too, after suffering traumatic experiences in the Franco-Prussian War, announced his engagement to an-other English girl, Fanny Knipe, his aunt's cousin and companion. After their honeymoon they took up residence in Montparnasse House, near the walls of Dinan. Some years later they moved to La Voliere in rue Aristide Briand, a minute or two from the English church.

Cosme kept detailed diaries from which we learn that he was a more than conventionally religious man. When in Paris he would drop into a convenient church for private prayer and often held services at home. He was an early ecumenist and frequently attended Roman Catholic services, encouraging his children to join in the festivals and processions on holy days. He and his wife also attended the Église Reformée and at one time he was a member of the Presbyteral Council at Rennes. No one thought there was anything strange about such activities by an Anglican churchwarden.

Cosme accepted the role of churchwarden out of a sense

of duty, rather than inclination. 'I received a long and very flattering letter from Mr Orger in which he pressed me to accept the functions of churchwarden. I can see well that I cannot avoid it any longer and that I must take it on from poor General Hope.' By then he had been a member of the committee for ten years and it was perceived that the changing circumstances of French Law after the events of 1870 demanded a churchwarden well-versed in legal matters.

During his term of office he managed a successful project to establish a Girls High School which, under its headmistresses Miss Brown and Miss McCullum, was to enjoy a successful existence until it became the Girls Lycee. There was no parallel boys' school as their brothers were sent home to English boarding schools. It was Cosme who undertook the legal work for the school to gain recognition from the authorities just as he succeeded in reducing the tax levy on the church property. As a non-recognised religion in France the Anglican 'temple' was subject to the same tax laws as commercial businesses. At this time in Dinan a considerable amount of bad feeling grew up between the English and French residents and it was up to the churchwardens to restore good relations. The eirenic de Satge acted with commendable tact, especially when reports of Englishmen behaving badly hit the headlines. Amongst other problems he faced were cases of bad debt, a British officer caught poaching and when the August Club, of which Cosme was so proud to have been elected a member, was raided by the police for illicit gambling.

However, strong and cohesive as the English community in Dinan was, it is evident that, because they did not own or feel any ultimate responsibility for their church, they did not learn to love it in the way of many parishes in England. All financial and administrative control was in the hands of SPG in London. With the growing popularity of Dinard for the wealthier people, the English community began to decline almost from the moment of the building of the church. There were several cases of poverty amongst the remaining English and bad debts continued to increase towards the end of the century. The withering away of the community led also to cases of extreme loneliness amongst the British who could not hold a conversation in French, and quite a number took to drink. The church building was never fully completed and ambitious plans to purchase a new organ as well as to find new money to pay the chaplain had to be abandoned.

Perhaps the most bitter disappointment for De Satge came when Bishop Wilkinson (responsible for North and Central Europe) refused to go to Dinan for the confirmation of his children, Beatrice and Philippe. 'Candidates must go to Dinard.' 'A most unfortunate decision,' recorded Cosme on 18th February 1894, 'We were so looking forward to seeing [them] confirmed in our lovely little church, where they received their baptism.'

Shortly after this, the chaplain,the Reverend G. Orger resigned and the new chaplain, appointed from London by SPG, did not fit into the community. Trouble and friction were to follow. Cosme de Satge, now a weary man, found the function of peacemaker too demanding. He was now the victim of failing health and increasing financial difficulties and, at the Annual Meeting of 1897 handed over his responsibilities to Admiral Sullivan. Satge's last recorded ecclesiastical note in his diary found on 20th June 1897: 'To church at 11 o'clock with all the family. The decorations make a good display. Special hymns in honour of Queen Victoria's Diamond Jubilee.'

A month later, the chaplain, Dr Stanley also announced his resignation, although he was to continue close links with the area until he was drowned when the cross channel steamer, the St Hilda, went down in 1905. Christ Church, Dinan was doomed and, although it struggled on intermittently, became disused and deserted by the Second World War. Shortly after that the present writer found it forlorn and broken, a solitary reminder of a thriving community now vanished and come to dust.

Before the eventual sale of Christ Church, Dinan however, the Committee of the well-established Anglican church at Dinard took responsibility for it and paid out considerable sums of money to keep the church building in good repair. They also paid the cost of insurance at a rate of 424.24 Francs per annum for six years. When the town of Dinan offered to purchase the site of the church on 31st January, 1973, the President of the Dinard Association, Mr Bill Channing, wrote to Canon Isherwood at USPG on 10th February 1973 to the effect that 'both the previous Bishops of Fulham, Roger Coote and Alan Rogers stated that any monies gained from the sale of the property at Dinan, could be used by St Bartholomew's for so long as it was operating as a church but should revert to the Bishop of Fulham if at any time St Bartholomew's ceased to function as a church. This together with war reparations given to the church in the 1950s would help to keep an important physical presence for the Church of England in this area of France.'

Harold Isherwood appeared at first to accept the claim, and wrote to the diocese and USPG confirming 'that the British American Church of Dinard, France is a recognised Anglican Church and is in the diocese of the Bishop of Fulham and Gibraltar. Apart from the collections of the faithful, they have no other support. Some members and friends of the church occasionally make small annual contributions. The church can be considered for all purposes as a charitable institution.'

Alas, although Dinan church was sold to the town for 10,000 Francs, Bill Channing was informed that 'the capital belongs to the diocese and will be invested for the benefit of local churches.' Although by this time, St Bartholomew's was the last remaining Anglican church in the whole area, no money was to be forthcoming.

The Chapels of St Malo

The founding of the churches in the port districts of St Malo, St Servan and Paramé followed a rather different pattern and was based on differently perceived ideas. In the manner of Mr Lechmere's letter from Guingamp, the British Vice Consul in St Malo wrote to the Continental Chaplains Committee on 20th July 1863 and again on 30th September announcing that he had 'rented a chapel at St Malo and proposes to build one in Dinard.' He requested that SPG should contribute towards the chaplain's salary for St Malo and Dinard on the grounds that there were 'at least thirty poor residents and always sixty to seventy British sailors without any spiritual provision, the chapel at St Servan being so distant and inconveniently situated, that no sailors attend it.'

In reply the committee wrote that 'St Servan is nearer the port of St Malo than Dinard' and that 'the residents of Dinard are too few to warrant a grant'. It turned out that their decision was based on a recent visit by the Bishop of Winchester. It was a momentous one for the people of Dinard to whom it was made clear that no money would be forthcoming from church sources to help them to build a church although every other British community in the region would receive considerable support, at the cost of allowing their property and administration to be overseen from London. Dinard would have to go it alone, and it could hardly have been foreseen that the church there, founded and built by laymen, with no encouragement or assistance from diocesan or other official bodies, would outlive all the other chaplaincies.

Meanwhile Mr Monteith maintained his efforts to obtain

assistance for St Malo, and the Committee received a letter from him with two clergymen, the Reverends F. Fitzgerald and W. P. Cobbe as co-signatories, continuing to argue that St Servan was inaccessible to sailors and that a chaplaincy and chapel were recommended for St Malo. The Committee agreed to this and a grant was made on 16th December 1863 for the coming year. (A handwritten note on the history of St Malo and Paramé churches claims that £40 per annum was donated in 1859 and 1862 but there is no record of this in SPG documents.) Unfortunately it was revealed on 4th November 1864, that the appointed chaplain, the Reverend L. Bickerstaffe had failed to supply satisfactory testimonials and had thus not been licensed so the grant was not paid. The Reverend W. P. Cobbe, who was to play a formative role in the establishment of the Dinard chaplaincy, was appointed chaplain of St Malo in his place. Mr Cobbe lived with Mr Monteith and services were held at his house.

The support given by SPG included a box of church materials comprising a surplice, Bible, prayer books, hymn books, altar linen, alms dish, vessels for the Holy Communion, supplied by the London jeweller Mr J. Keith, and a chant book for the psalms. The chaplain was expected to provide a second surplice from his own resources. In official letters Mr Cobbe was described as 'chaplain of St Malo and Dinard' but there were again hesitations about his status and the SPG grant was withheld in 1865 and 1866. Apparently the Bishop of London had withheld his permission to officiate and a letter jointly signed by Mr Monteith and the Reverend W. P. Cobbe admits that 'no chaplain can be helped if he does not hold the Bishop of London's licence.' This memo from St Malo casts doubt on the measure of Episcopal recognition accorded to the venture and there was certainly a vacancy in the 1860s until the Reverend H. B. (W. in the St Malo notes) Snooke took over the chaplaincy which was 'then transferred to Dinard about 1869'. But there were further problems for Snooke resigned in 1869. Possibly, he had never been licensed, for on 17th December 1866 the Bishop of London had written to the Continental Chaplains Committee to say that '[he] will not for the moment interfere with the services contemplated by the Reverend H. B. Snooke at St Malo on the recommendation of the Society (SPG) but reserves [his] official sanction and licence until such time as may be thought proper between the Foreign Office and [himself].' Mention of the Foreign Office reveals the arm of the Established Church and the interest taken in it by government.

Whether licenced or not, Snooke did a good job in St Malo, for in the room rented at the corner of the rue de Toulouse, numbers attending divine worship increased dramatically. SPG continued to make grants of £40 per annum and on 12th May 1868 a grant was requested towards the maintenance of the rented room.

When the Reverend H. B. Snooke resigned, he remained in the area, perhaps hoping to be appointed chaplain of the proposed church in Dinard. The St Malo chaplaincy remained empty until 1876 when the Reverend Edward Davidson rented a small room in the rue du Puits Abray and then leased a building at the back of 14, rue de Dinan which he then fitted up as a chapel. It had been a warehouse and had a seating capacity for 120 persons, 'possessing an oak-timbered roof which lent an ecclesiastical appearance to the room, when properly fitted up with an altar, hangings at the east end, choir seats etc.'

Davidson was followed in 1887 by the Reverend James Stapleton Cotton when the chapel was completely vested in SPG who made annual grants until its final closure in 1897. Earlier in its history the Continental Chaplains Committee had wisely suggested that the chapel should be taken over by a body of local Trustees. Had this been done, there is a chance that it would have survived in the way

St Bartholomew's, Dinard survived with its active and responsible local Trustees. Throughout the twentieth century in England, private patrons and villagers have been demoralised to see their beloved church made redundant by diocesan authorities anxious to make ends meet and reluctant to relinquish control to local people. How much more did this affect the more loosely regulated Anglican churches in France.

Paramé Church

While chaplain of St Malo, Mr Davidson had drawn up a plan for a permanent church building to be built outside the walls of St Malo on the 'Sillon', conveniently situated 'for the English sailors and traders whose, vessels when on shore, would be close at hand.' But since 'Mr Davidson's resignation a colony of English had sprung up and fairly taken root at Paramé.' It was confidently anticipated that the resort would speedily develop, not only during the summer months but even for the winter and spring seasons. This was an obvious site for an Anglican church, especially in view of the fact as stated in a letter to SPG in London that 'the congregation from Paramé crowd out the British sailors for whom St Malo church was originally intended and that the English people living in Paramé find it impossible to send their children to church on account of the distance and expense of the tramways.'

Perhaps a more telling argument was that the 'seafaring classes and the commercial element' in the town 'were known to be nonconformists and as such would certainly not support a new Anglican church even if it were brought to their doors.' There was a Meeting House for Sunday worship already in place at 'The Sailors' Rest' in St Malo where services were conducted by a layman on Nonconformist lines. Why then should a new church be built in a situation where it would certainly fail to be appreciated by 'those whose interests lay rather in the direction of Nonconformity and where, at the same time, it would be furthest away from those whose pockets would be taxed most heavily to support it and who were most eager to enjoy those spiritual privileges which it could afford'? It was also pointed out that many of the people of Paramé already attended the church in Dinan in large numbers.

Matters were brought to a head at the end of 1892 when an anonymous resident of Paramé bought a piece of land in the Avenue Duguay Frossin and offered it for the use of a new church. Building began on 4th January 1893 from designs prepared by M. Pariset, architect of St Servan. As was usual at this time, permission had to be sought from the local Roman Catholic Archbishop and, as in Dinan and elsewhere, a solemn pledge was made that the 'temple' should be used solely for worship by the British colony and that nothing in the nature of 'propaganda' should ever be attempted amongst the French. So rapid was the building that the opening service of dedication was held on the 22nd June 1894. This seems to have been a local initiative as decisions were made continually in the Continental Chaplaincies Committee, now firmly controlled by SPG, to defer building until universal agreement had been reached.

The building of the church could not have gone ahead without the considerable support of forty-three local contributors who provided 18,750 Francs and the round of coffee mornings, concerts and bazaars which provided a further 3860 Francs. SPG eventually gave a loan of 10,000 Francs to be repaid over five years. Of the initial contributors were eight soldiers, three of whom were generals, a large number of widows including Mrs Kitchener, mother of the Field Marshal, ten clergy, three doctors and additional donations from Crosse and Blackwell and Huntley and Palmer.

The Reverend John Dunn became chaplain for a brief time

until he became chaplain at St Servan which managed to maintain a separate existence for some time and Paramé was without a priest until SPG appointed a former chaplain of St Malo, the Reverend R. Sinclair Kendall in 1899. His stay was a short one of only one year but he returned in March 1915 to see the church through the war and its aftermath until 1923. SPG regularly told the chaplains that their main work must be amongst the sailors of St Malo and failure in this area would mean the withdrawal of their grant.

There was an experiment to run the churches at St Servan and Paramé jointly after the First World War but this 'was only moderately successful as neither church could have full services and not likely to be repeated by SPG.' Parishioners and parochial clergy at the end of the twentieth century are permitted to be mystified by this announcement in days when they are frequently sharing a group of up to twelve village churches, at considerable distances from each other and still managing a degree of pastoral care! However there was an advance in 1920 when the Sailors Rest, 'for several years past carried on privately by Mr Harrison, British Vice Consul, was incorporated into the work of the chaplaincy and the chaplain became chairman.'

Paramé church was improved in 1922 when War Memorial windows were placed in the nave and a Rose window at the West End. These were the design and work of Messrs Deschamps of Dol while another 'beautiful and costly Memorial window', donated by Mrs Annie Webb in memory of her grandson, Thomas Sanders, was designed and executed by Miss Frye of Cambridge, Masschusetts. This was in place over the altar at the East End by Advent 1924, the principal motif being Christ the Good Shepherd receiving and blessing children. M. Deschamps personally came to fit the window and, at the same time, the whole church was redecorated. At the subsequent dedication of the windows, it was reported that 'the bishop preached a most stirring sermon.'

An ominous moment for Paramé church and the others in Europe controlled by SPG, came when the Bishop of Gibraltar announced on 29th December 1919 that regular collections must be given to SPG under whose control they were allowed to exist. This centralisation became a major cause of the collapse and closure of churches in the twentieth century when times became more difficult, for there was no local person who felt fully responsible for their maintenance and upkeep.

It has to be said that Paramé church suffered from the type of organisation beloved of bureaucrats, especially those acting from a distance. It became an established practice that the church treasurer should be the British Vice Consul at St Malo who was usually the local manager of the Southern (formerly South West) Railway depot in the port. He changed every three years or so and the role of treasurer was handed on from person to person. It is not known whether the Railway authorities selected the manager on account of his being a good churchman but it does illustrate one facet of the operation of an established church. This arrangement lasted until after the Second World War when the church reopened after extensive restoration made necessary by the bombing of St Malo by the RAF.

The French Ministry of Reconstruction paid the first two million Francs toward the restoration of war damage after which it contributed seventy per cent of the costs. Protracted negotiations by the Reverend Dr Hillyard and SPG resulted in extensive and excellent repair work and services on a limited basis from July to September took place, attracting only modest congregations.

Dr Hillyard, a retired priest, was responsible for most of the local administration and SPG, who owned the church, had to find some £750 to make the church finally fit for worship. Whether or not this came from the proceeds of the sale of St Servan is not clear from Mr Dudley Dixon's letter from the Society. There is a reference to 549,000 Francs from the sale of St Servan going toward the total cost of 2,457, 079 Francs. Dr Hillyard died in March 1951, before the date of completion but the redoubtable Mrs Hillyard immediately wrote to SPG on 20th March to say that she 'would be keeping an eye on the workmen.' Soon afterwards Bishop G. C. Chambers, chaplain at the British Embassy in Paris from 1947 to 1955, came to rededicate the church. 'I left Paris on Friday morning, July 4th, by the 8.55 train, arriving at St Malo sometime after 2.0 p.m. Miss Hannay from Dinard met me ... I am delighted to find the church so well restored ... the service of hallowing which I took at 6.00 p.m.' Of course everyone at St Bartholomew's, Dinard knows that Elizabeth Hannay was responsible for keeping the Anglican faith going in post-war Brittany and this is but one example of how she took a positive, guiding interest in the remaining churches in the area, not least in St Bartholomew's which owes its existence to her. The fact was that there was no longer any British colony in Paramé and the church depended entirely on summer visitors.

The church in Paramé never recovered from the effects of the war and the departure of the British. For a few years summer chaplains came to do duty from July to mid-September. SPG paid them three guineas per Sunday but chaplains protested at the expense and difficulty of the visits. One problem affecting all visitors was that for many years after the war the British government allowed tourists only £25 per passport to be taken abroad. One chaplain, the Reverend C. H. D. Grimes of Newton Abbott pointed out that this severely limited the length of time which could be spent there.

The registers reveal that the average number of communicants during the short season was between five and eight, while attendance at Morning Prayer depended on groups of Girl Guides from a local camp site and school parties. There was no indigenous congregation.

Interest in the church revived in 1959 when the Continental Chaplaincies Committee received a letter from Pasteur J. C. Guillaume of the Église Reformée in St Malo ...'We have not been able to find a building for our services. We thought therefore that you would perhaps allow us to hold regular services during the months when it is closed. Our aim is to make our French people acquainted with the Holy Scriptures and let them know Jesus Christ as their personal Saviour. We would be very glad to see this beautiful, but now deserted church fulfil its purpose ..'

Shortly after, the Anglican Church ended its connexion with Paramé.

Trinity Church, St Servan

The little church at St Servan had been the first Anglican church to be erected in the St Malo district but was another direct casualty of the Second World War, although no services had been held there for some years before. It had a succession of chaplains up to the 1920s. One of these was the Reverend W. Money who was one of the clergy reported to have attended the first service to be held on the site of St Bartholomew's, Dinard.

The church's most auspicious moment came when negotiations for its sale were being carried out, at the time when Elizabeth Hannay at St Bartholomew's was pioneering the ecumenical work in the area. Pasteur Forget, who was allowed to use the deserted Anglican church at Dinan, showed a willingness to buy the closed church at St Servan in 1950. He also offered a loan for the reconstruction of Parame church until the Ministry of Reconstruction paid up. Negotiations were undertaken with the Reverend Dr Hillyard who, as we have seen was largely responsible for the successful completion of the restoration of the church at Paramé, and they seemed to be going well. But the good Pasteur was also in touch with the Bishop of Fulham through a French agent, about the possible purchase of the church in Dinan. Dr Hillyard found out about this and was incensed that he was being by-passed by London. He wrote a furious letter to Mr Dudley Dixon and SPG, claiming that the Bishop of Fulham had insulted him by going behind his back by dealing directly with Pasteur Forget, and promptly resigned. 'Mr Forget has acted crookedly,' he wrote. 'First he made a definite offer of 600,000 Francs. Afterwards he withdrew his offer and threatened that he would demand the church for nothing as he had found a clause in the French Code to that effect.'

In the event, Pasteur Forget did not get his way. The church was sold by the diocese for 500,000 Francs to a private individual and relations between the Bishop and Dr Hillyard were restored.

St Lunaire

St Lunaire features prominently in the life of St Bartholomew's for the Bishop of London wrote to the committee of the church asking them to provide financial and pastoral support for the services at St Enogat and St Lunaire. The result was that the Reverend Mr Harper was taken on as a locum chaplain under the supervision of the chaplain at Dinard, by agreement of St Bartholomew's committee on 5th April 1905. The committee noted at the same time, that the ground promised for the erection of a chapel of ease should be secured in *propria firma* and an endowment be made to provide funds for its erection at St Lunaire during the season. The arrangement suited the chaplain at Dinard for, once having appointed 'a desirable clergyman and good preacher for the services at St Enogat and St Lunaire,' he arranged that he should be transferred to Dinard 'during the chaplain's holiday at the charge of church funds, which was to be thirty guineas.'

On 23rd April 1906, the committee again discussed a proposal by the Bishop that they should apply to SPG for funds to build the church and that the Society should acquire the sole appointment of the chaplain. One of the committee, Mr Spencer Chapman agreed to advance £200 at 4 per cent per annum, provided the church was completed. The Revd Harper who remained locum chaplain at St Lunaire, accepted the offer from M. Laraque of a good site for a 'chapel of ease at Dinard' at St Lunaire but the Dinard Committee requested that Mr Harper should also ask for a donation of 2500 Francs as a gift towards the building of the chapel. SPG and the Bishop of Northern and Central Europe, suffragan to the Bishop of London, were informed and by June 1906, plans from the architect had been received. The Committee of St Bartholomew's ruled that the cost of the building should not exceed 12,000 Francs.

The little church at St Lunaire survived as a place of worship until 1938 when it closed partly on account of the difficulty of finding locum chaplains during the summer season. It had never opened throughout the year and, once the building and the appointment of chaplains was taken over by SPG, the committee of St Bartholomew's lost interest in it.

During the First World War, it is recorded by the Continental Chaplaincies Committee that St Lunaire Church was used by French Protestant soldiers for services and was 'otherwise unused.'

At the end of the Second World War, a member of the Dinard committee, Mrs Forbes, visited the church and wrote a report to SPG that 'it was a nice brick building' but she 'could not gain access as no one has seen the key since the war ended.' It looked in good repair however. Obviously the local French people did not regard it as a place of worship as, she continued in her report, that 'there was a request from a neighbour to use the church as a chicken run, while another old lady wanted to squat on the church land.'

SPG however persevered and opened the church during two months of the summer season. This continued for some years for the Reverend J. D. Weston, who acted as a sort of SPG inspector, wrote in 1957 that 'the chaplaincies of Paramé and St Lunaire seem to go well. From St Lunaire I heard that Mr Clark found the church door forced and open ... a poor owl and another bird had got into the church and could not escape, resulting in one mangled carcass and one dead owl.' I wonder what Mr Weston's criteria were for a church 'going badly?'

Conclusion

Five churches have been surveyed, all of which lasted less than one hundred years. One of their problems was that they were controlled and financed from a distant diocesan centre and SPG, both in London and they lacked the people who had a personal love and interest in their church. The Society which owned them and the committee which ran them inevitably had a prior concern for the careful steward-ship of their funds, yet showed a reluctance shared by most committees, to delegate responsibility and control. Local Anglicans watched the demise of their churches with con-cern and one member of St Bartholomew's, Dinard expressed his anxieties in a letter written at a time when his church was in difficulties in 1924; 'it might become like other churches in the district, just as another church in Dinard has become a bazaar or like the old church at St Malo which has become a furniture warehouse'.

These churches and others in the region, like St Peter's

Avranches were built on sand without the solid foundations of a responsible and caring congregation. It is thanks to faithful Christians and good churchmen like Sir George Curtis, Elizabeth Hannay and others, that the independent but loyal Anglican church of St Bartholomew's Dinard survived through some very difficult years and remains the only building still witnessing to the Anglican faith in Brittany today.

CHAPTER THREE

The House on the Rock: the Foundation of St Bartholomew's, Dinard

The brief survey of the Anglican churches in North Brittany helps to illustrate the size of the English-speaking population and the zeal for building places of worship to supply the spiritual needs of the people. However it is one thing to build a church and quite another to maintain it when times are hard and it is a tribute to the many local people in Dinard that St Bartholomew's still stands and serves a large congregation with services every day of the week. A clear lesson to be learned from the other foundations is that a church cannot be managed at a distance, and events have shown that the church in Dinard was wise to remain independent and under the management and administration of local trustees. Even then the management has never been completely free of problems and anxiety.

Before St Bartholomew's became a reality, the Continental Chaplaincies Committee working under the auspices of SPG were resolute in their affirmation that there was no perceived need for a church in Dinard while there was one in St Malo. The Reverends W. P. Cobbe and H. B. Snooke styled themselves 'chaplain of St Malo and Dinard' during the 1860s, and it is possible that both chaplains visited Dinard to take services in the existing, handsomely constructed English-speaking church. This still stands in the rue Jacques Cartier (formerly rue du Temple), clearly an ecclesiastical building but now serving as a curio shop. This 'temple' may have been built by American residents to serve the free church communities for there are no service registers, baptismal records or any other records relating to the worship there and there is no mention of it in any of the diocesan records in London. It must have enjoyed a very brief existence as a church for, as we shall see, the congregation soon abandoned it for the newly founded St Bartholomew's.

The vision and inspiration for the church of St Bartholomew belongs to Mrs Lyona Faber and, years later, in the 1920s, her grand-daughter wrote a brief description of how it came about. Apart from one or two minor details, Mrs Lyona H. Hody's memory served her well:

> My grandmother, Mrs Lyona Johanna Faber, after the death of her husband, William Faber at Dinard in 1854, bought in 1856 or 1857, land at Dinard stretching from the sea front in front of a Bric a Brac shop to the rue Coppinger comprising what is now the rue des Cedres and all the land on each side of it. The southern boundary was the street in front of the Hotel des Dunes. She built St Catherine's in 1857. She died in 1866 and left the property to her son William Stanley Faber who gave the land to the Church in her memory – and began building it in about 1874. It was more expensive than he expected and was finished by contributions given by English people interested in Dinard – After her brother's death my mother [Mrs Hody Cox] had the gift of the living until about 1890 when she handed it over to a committee. I think the church was under the jurisdiction of the Bishop of Fulham and the Bishop of North and Central Europe. Bishop Berry [sic] held a confirmation there not long before the last war – William Stanley Faber built several houses in the rue des Cedres including the Villa du Jardin. He sold the land on which Roche Corneille and Staplefield were afterward built – The street up the hill past the Church was called rue Faber after my grandfather. I

believe they changed the name after the last war – my grand-
mother planted the cedar trees in the rue des Cedres. My
grandparents and parents were buried in St Enogat
cemetery.' Lyona H. Hody.

At Ladraw House
S. Devon.

In fact there is compelling evidence that Mrs Lyona Faber
intended the church to be built as a memorial to her
husband and her son probably added her name. There is a
memorial to both in the church.

At first the building of the church was a private family
enterprise, as was the case with many churches in England
and Wales at this time, and the family retained the 'gift' of
the living for some years. However it is evident that, from
the first it was intended to be an Anglican (Episcopalian)
church for application was made to the bishop of London
for a priest to be licensed to officiate in the chaplaincy of
Dinard. This application resulted in the appointment and
the Bishop of London's permission on 9th Dec 1873, for
'the Reverend Anthony Thomson to perform the office of
Chaplain to the British residents worshipping in the chapel
belonging to W. Stanley Faber Esquire situate at Dinard in
France as long as the appointment of the said W. Stanley
Faber continues in force and no longer'

Mr Thomson was already a priest in France and came
from Avranches where he had run a school, training boys for
a military career. When he arrived in Dinard he opened a
school for boys at the Villa Beausejour and wrote a book,
based on his experiences entitled *The English School Room*.
One of his four sons and two daughters, Noel, wrote a
popular guide book on Brittany before retiring to Guernsey,
having married the daughter of Admiral Ingles.

Unfortunately, little is now known of these early days of
St Bartholomew's church but it is recorded that the nave of
the church was completed by the time of the arrival of the

Reverend A. Thomson in 1873. While the author was search-
ing around the church for material, he recently found the
original designs for the construction of the present church
dated 1869 by M. Faber, now in a very delapidated condition,
having lain under the organ for some considerable time.
These plans were executed exactly as proposed and it is
possible that it had been hoped to complete the building of
the church to coincide with the planned visit of the Empress
Eugenie to Dinard in 1870. The Franco Prussian War of
that year and the subsequent collapse of the Empire undoubtedly affected the plans and caused some delay.

The first person to be baptised in the newly constructed
church was Oliver Henry North on 3rd June 1874 and the
first recorded funeral service is that of a three-year old,
Robert Sturges Thorndike some six days later. During Mr
Thomson's time as chaplain, it appears that he did not keep
a regular service register and noted the 'occasional' offices
in a school exercise book. These were transferred to a formal
register by the Reverend R. Peck when he became chaplain
in 1890.

The early registers reveal the strength of the community
and the families who were attracted to Dinard. Among the
declared occupations were a majority of 'gentlemen' and
army officers but a handful of ex-Indian Civil Service em-
ployees and other colonial servants including an Inspector
of Constabulary from Fiji, a civil engineer, a doctor, farmer,
teachers, a carpenter, a brick-maker, a single woman and a
good number of domestic servants. One of the carpenters
to be married, whose family was to play such an important
role in St Bartholomew's for one hundred years, was Samuel
Edward Clark, a widower, who married a widow, Lydia
Hamilton, on 23rd February 1891. His son by his previous
marriage, John Albert Clark married Helen Maud Hameth
on 22nd October 1910, having been previously baptised and
confirmed in the church. Clark senior was church verger

from 1871 to 1915 when his son took over from him to serve for the next 45 years. There are fitting memorials to their long service in the church today.

The Reverend Anthony Thomson stayed only sufficiently long to ensure that the church was becoming known to the new British and American residents and an established pattern of regular worship was taking place. He retired to Guernsey to join his family. In his place the Bishop of London gave the Reverend Arthur Keville Davies Edwards, BA, permission to perform the office of chaplain to the British residents at Dinard on 19th October 1877.

Already it was found that the church was too small for the growing congregation and by 4th April 1877 fresh plans had been drawn up by the architects who had produced the original plans for the church. This included adding the Eastern Transept as well as the North Aisle parallel to the Nave. These were accepted by William Faber who was still the sole proprietor of the church and we still possess the detailed specifications for the South (Western) Transept, signed by M. Liege, the architect, and Mr Faber, which stated that the extension should be started immediately and completed by 1st July with the demolition of the now interior wall (running from the pulpit to the children's window today) being completed by 7th July 1878. At the same time, most of the furniture and fittings familiar to us today were installed and there is a receipt from Cox and Sons in London relating to church items purchased from then, including alms dishes with velvet pads, an oak reading desk, a credence table, alms chest and wrought iron standards.

At the same time as this extension, or perhaps a little after, an ambitious new plan for the church was proposed by Mr Charles Walker, an architect from 26, Eldon Square, Newcastle-on-Tyne. While keeping the internal columns and roof much as it was, he proposed a totally new arrangement for the church, demolishing the South Porch entrance and

The Reverend Arthur Keville Davies Edwards, Chaplain of St
Bartholomew's, 1887–89. During his time the church was completed
more or less as we know it today, and dedicated.

building a new porch at the West End with entrances from each side. The font was to be placed up at the East End by the altar and adjacent to the vestry door while the enlarged vestry would have its own porch. The advantage of this plan was that it would increase the accommodation still further as well as giving the church a pleasing symmetrical appearance both inside and outside.

No records remain of any consideration of this plan but it is likely that Mr Faber rejected it on account of the cost. Finances were already bearing heavily upon him and he was forced to raise a subscription to raise the necessary funds while he himself was prepared only to offer a temporary loan for the enlargement of the church, though of course he was still the sole owner under French law.

At the request of Mr George Marshall, acting chairman of the Church Committee in 1891, the honorary secretary and churchwarden, Mr William Forbes, compiled a history of the church to date, confirming the above dates and adding that the church was dedicated by the Bishop of Derry (Berry) in 1880. There is no record of this apart from his note and it is difficult to be certain of the identity of the bishop, unless it is a mistaken spelling of Bishop Bury, then suffragan to the Bishop of London and responsible for North & Central Europe. There was a later controversy about whether or not the church had been consecrated and, although a later bishop stated categorically that it had been, thus altering its constitutional and material status, there is no mention of such consecration in the Bishop of London's Acts Book. Usually for a consecration there is a record of the petition and its acceptance as well as the act of consecration itself. None of these are evident in diocesan records.

An Unsolved Mystery

We have seen in the last chapter that two English chaplains, the Reverend W. P. Cobbe and the Reverend H. B. Snooke styled themselves chaplains of St Malo and Dinard and were also occasionally referred to as such in the minutes of the Continental Chaplaincies Committee in the 1860s. In the register of Baptisms and Marriages at St Malo, there is a note, dated 16th November 1871, that 'The new Church built by Mr Faber Esq., was opened for Divine Service by Mr Money of St Servan, Mr Bird of Foulsham, Norfolk and the Rev. H. B. Snooke at 11 o'clock a.m. on Thursday, Nov. 16th 1871 – The sermon being preached by the latter from Psalm 122 v 1 "I was glad when they said unto me, We will go into the House of the Lord" – There was a collection after the service.'

This date has been accepted as the foundation date or the opening for worship of St Bartholomew's and, indeed, the hundredth anniversary was celebrated in 1971. But we now know that the church building was delayed and that the central Nave and altar had not been built until 1873 while the other transepts were constructed in 1877 and 1878.

At St Malo Mr Snooke had been meticulous in keeping the registers, yet he did not leave any records of other services taking place in Dinard after this introductory one. The service on 16th November may have taken place in the other American Protestant church in the rue du Temple which, as we shall see, had a short life. M. Fermin, curator of the Museum in Dinard and the expert on the history of Dinard, suggests it was a building for what the British call nonconformist worship, built by the American colony. A better date for the foundation Mr Faber's church may be 24th August, St Bartholomew's Day, 1873, although services had taken place at least occasionally for a few weeks before then.

The Congregations Unite in Dinard

Even during the 1870s when the British and American population was increasing rapidly, it was obvious that the community would not be able to sustain two churches and it fell to the new chaplain to attempt to unite the congregations. It could not have been easy for a group of people who had contributed and worked hard to erect their building and understandably felt a pride in their achievement. Today the precise details of the situation are no longer known, nor do we know quite how the situation was resolved but a testimonial letter from the American Consul General indicates the geniality and tact by which the Reverend Arthur Edwards achieved the aim of uniting the congregations. After twelve years in Dinard he applied to become chaplain of the English Church at Lausanne in Switzerland. The Consul General supported his application with the following letter:

To the members of the English Church at Lausanne
Dinard 9th.I.89

Gentlemen,
I have great pleasure in bearing testimony to the wise considerateness and tact with which the Revd. A. K. Edwards has invariably dealt with his congregation at Dinard.

The position at the commencement of his ministrations there was a difficult one, as the congregations had divided and two rival churches had been built soon after Mr Edward's arrival – the second church was closed and since that time no shadow of disturbance or trouble has arisen; and yet the congregation is composed of Americans and English with very many different opinions.

Mr Edwards leaving Dinard will be a matter of regret to his American and to his English friends.

I do not see that under the circumstances I could say more in Mr Edwards's favour; if I did I would say it.

Your obedt. Servant,

Ray Moultry
U. S. Consular General

Church parade during La Belle Époque, c.1904.
(*Collections Henri Fermin*)

St Bartholomew's Church had overcome its first challenge in its early years. Perhaps the reason for the necessity of extending the church so dramatically within five years of its original building was the large influx of congregation from the other church which caused Mr Faber to go beyond his budget. It soon became clear to him that he could not continue to be personally responsible for the upkeep and maintenance of the church and all the administration that went with it. In 1882, when almost all the debt owing to him had been fully paid, thanks largely to the generous donations of Sir Philip Egerton (his memorial is in the window in the chancel behind the priest's stall), Mr Faber took steps to hand the property to a board of Trustees.

Without seeking help from any outside source, St Bartholomew's rapidly become the recognised English and American church of the area, large enough to seat the substantial numbers of summer visitors as well as the local residents and accepted by the Bishop of London as part of his responsibility and jurisdiction. Mr Faber and the Trustees who followed him retained the ownership and patronage of the property but were, from the start, meticulous in appointing only those chaplains to whom the bishop was prepared to give permission to officiate.

But why St Bartholomew's?

One last question from its foundation remains. How and why was its dedication to St Bartholomew chosen? In England he is not a particularly popular saint and little is known of his life.

It is possible that St Bartholomew meant something to the Faber family, either through the dedication of their home church in England or through some connection with the great hospital in London or some other institution.

Perhaps it was the fortuitously chosen date for the turning

of the first clod of earth for the foundations or the laying of the foundation stone but, if so, one would expect the moment to have been marked in some way.

A more romantic suggestion is that the name was chosen at a time when Anglicans were much happier about being described as Protestants than they are today. Thus they saw, in the building of their church, an opportunity of reminding their French Catholic neighbours of the horrific massacre of their fellow Protestants on St Bartholomew's Day in 1571 when thousands of Huguenots were murdered throughout France. The initial poignancy and infamy of the day lived on through the centuries until the greater crimes of the twentieth century dulled man's memory. What better way could British residents living abroad show their loyalty to her Imperial Majesty Queen Victoria, mother of all the crowned Protestant heads of Europe, than to express their own Protestant loyalty in such forthright terms?

However a more straightforward explanation for the choice may be the simple fact that, of all the major saints days, St Bartholomew's comes at the height of the summer season when the largest number of visitors might be in Dinard and his Feast of Dedication could be worthily celebrated and attended.

For the moment the reason for the dedication is unknown to us. It may have been the combination of two or three ideas and, in the meantime, we are permitted to speculate on our favourite choice.

CHAPTER FOUR

Consolidation and Development under the Trust, 1882–1914

Transfer of Ownership

In French law, the church and the land on which it was built was still the absolute private property of Mr William Stanley Faber, although it was now being administered by his son-in-law Captain Hody Cox. Mr Faber was forced to ask for donations to maintain and extend the building, while he offered money on loan to be repaid in six-monthly instalments.

By 1882, most of the loan had been repaid and, acting on behalf of Mr Faber, Captain Hody Cox proceeded with the transfer of the property to a committee of 'Trustees' who were to look after it on an informal basis until more satisfactory arrangements could be made. The first names 'to secure the church for the congregation' were Colonel Hamilton and Mr J. B. Camac but the names of Mr John Forster and the chief benefactor Sir Philip Grey Egerton were soon added on 2nd April and 16th October 1882. According to the historical record in the Committee minute book, dated January 1891, there was a deed of Trust drawn up by Captain Hody Cox on 8th October 1883 to ensure that Mr Faber's intentions would be carried out, including a commitment to guarantee the chaplain's salary of £150 per annum, but there is no trace of this document now.

Captain Hody Cox continued to reserve the appointment to the chaplaincy for himself until 10th April 1884 when he gave it over to the Trustees and the names of Captain the Hon. Albert Denison and Captain Richard Wells were added.

The first formal transfer of the property was enacted by a deed of 23rd May, and completed on 21st August 1884 when the site and building passed into the hands of the church trustees by a document of 'Vente par Mr Cox pour Mr Faber a Mr Grey Egerton et consorts du temple protestant de Dinard et du terrain sur lequel il est construit.' This was drawn up by M. Jean-Marie Fourmand, notaire of St Malo.

The sale of the property was for 5000 Francs 'which Mr Cox acting for Mr Faber recollects having received from the purchasers'. The purchasers, in addition to Sir Philip Egerton, consisted of three other 'Trustees'; Mr John Forster, George Marshall and Mr J. B. Camac, the only American citizen. Also included in the deed of sale were Captain Richard Wells, who was also acting on behalf of absentees in England, Colonel Hercules Rowley of London, Captain Albert Denison of Woodside, Wootton, Isle of Wight and Mr William Davy, living in Norfolk. According to the historical minute these were only included in the church transfer deed to act 'en cas de mort' and held no financial or management responsibility.

It is clear from the records of the proceedings kept by the Church Committee that the four purchasers regarded themselves as trustees on behalf of the congregation. But in fact there was nothing in the deed of sale to justify this. In French law they were the sole owners and had the sole liability. Strictly speaking, the law did not recognise the building as a church, for the Anglican faith remained a *religion inconnue* in French law and the four owners could have sold it legally at any time. There is no mention of any trust nor any conditions imposed regarding the uses to which the building might be put. The only condition imposed by the deed was the peculiar one, that the seven out of the eight purchasers mentioned in the deed who died first, should have no right to pass on their rights in the property to their heirs, but that the entire ownership of the property should devolve on the last survivor. In fact the last survivor would become the sole owner of St Bartholomew's Church and land. There were no restrictions in his power of transfer nor about the price he might ask for the property. He had full liberty under the deed to appropriate the whole proceeds of the sale for himself, if he so desired. He need not even maintain the building as a church and it was certainly was not necessary to maintain it as an Anglican church.

It was some years before the situation was fully appreciated and it caused difficulties and misunderstandings before it was resolved some forty years later.

The Committee at Work

St Bartholomew's has always been fortunate in having a hard-working and energetic committee of which the first presented an admirable example. From the start they took an active interest in church affairs, taking on for themselves many of the tasks left to the vicar or rector in England. By late 1884 they had sold the 'old' harmonium to Mr Moultry, the American Consul General and in 1885 had the church fully insured with British insurers for £3000. A note in February of that year also confirms that all remaining church debts to the bank and to the Trustees had been paid off.

The church secretary, Colonel H. Villiers Forbes, who was also churchwarden, kept meticulous records including a report of a meeting he had with Mr Faber 'on or about the last day he was in Dinard' which, he states, the Trustees are in honour bound to carry out, strictly in accordance with the wishes and intentions of the late Mr Faber as follows:

> That the Trustees should for ever and aye reserve to themselves the right of appointment of chaplains –
>
> That on no account should they elect a clergyman of extreme opinions and on no account let him be a Ritualist
>
> That the 'six months notice' should be strictly adhered to, any proposed alterations in Church should be referred to the Church Committee.

There was nothing particularly strange about these terms as they were similar to many parishes in England where the patron had the right of appointment to a living, while the bishop had the final word of approval by offering or withholding his licence. At this stage, however, it is clear that the terms of this Trust were quite informal and that, while the Trustees accepted a moral obligation to act on behalf of the congregation, they were under no legal obligation to observe them. In law they were simply owners of the land and property.

Little is now known of the final years of the incumbency of Arthur Edwards, although the church was increasingly well attended and by the time of his departure in 1889, all the necessary furniture and furnishings for a well-functioning church were in place. Mrs Villiers Forbes, the church organist, declined to accept her salary of 500 Francs per annum on condition that it be used to defray such church expenses 'as she may advisedly consider of some importance' and a number of significant gifts were donated by members of the congregation, which are still in evidence today.

The oak altar, six feet by three feet with carved legs was built in 1891, paid for out of the organist fund and the ladies of the church provided a white silk altar cloth, with Mrs Villiers Forbes and Mrs S. Chapman donating another. The

Hon. Mrs Marshall, who was to play a leading role in the future organisation of the church, donated the bronze cross while Mrs Beddingfield gave 'one carved rood' suggesting that, even in the earliest days of St Bartholomew's, 'ritualism' did not include ornaments normally associated with the more Tractarian forms of Anglicanism. Mrs Cuthbert gave the alms dishes and Lord Brassey donated the silver sacramental Cup and Chalice. Mrs Gordon gave the cushions for the altar rail together with a set of 'best stoles' and the Marchioness Hastings donated the carved oak chairs in the sanctuary, the brass lectern and the candlesticks with matching vases for the altar.

Gifts and memorials on such a scale as appears on the walls of St Bartholomew's, dating from this time indicates great faith in the church council and the future. And it was not too long before the committee were faced with their first real challenge in carrying out the terms of their Trust when it became necessary to appoint a new chaplain.

As patrons of the 'living' it seems that the Church Committee wished to hear applicants for the post of chaplain preach, as well as go through a form of interview, although this form of interview was one more commonly associated with the Free Churches. We do not know if this was the case in 1889 but the Reverend Richard Peck who was a Master of Arts of Cambridge University, seems to have satisfied the Trustees on all counts, including that of his moderate churchmanship, and was duly elected on the following terms:

His salary was to be 1000 Francs per Quarter and, in addition, he was to receive the church offerings six days each year including Easter and Christmas. The other days were the second Sunday each month from July to October when the congregations could be expected to be at their largest.

As a chaplain, Richard Peck did not enjoy the 'parson's

freehold' in the same way that incumbents in England and Wales could expect, but the terms of agreement included the clause that there was to be six months' notice given on the part of the chaplain or the Trustees 'in the event of any proposed change being contemplated in the matter of the chaplaincy or of the salary.'

The terms of Richard Peck's appointment must have satisfied the Bishop of London for he gave him his permission to officate at Dinard on 30th April 1890. From the moment of his arrival, the chaplain instituted full service registers which he kept meticulously and which are still in the church safe, and on each page stated that he held his 'licence to preach and officiate' from the Archbishop of Canterbury in addition to his 'permission' from the diocesan bishop. It may have been the policy at this time for chaplains in Europe and beyond to obtain a general licence from the Archbishop in the same manner as chaplains in the Royal Navy and Army on account of their regular moves overseas. Before he came to Dinard, the Reverend R. Peck had been chaplain at Versailles.

From Mr Peck's arrival the Church Committee, as it now preferred to be called, met regularly in the Club Room of the Dinard Club and included the chaplain. The members were not confined to the 'owners' of the church who had bought out Mr Faber in 1884 and they regularly added names to their list by invitation rather than by election by church members. On 16th May 1891, for example, J. Forster, Geo. Marshall, the Revd Richard Peck and Colonel Forbes as Hon. Secretary and Treasurer discussed the addition of Mr Spencer Chapman in place of Admiral Wells. Within the church membership this had some formal standing for 'there would be cause for the alteration to be made in the Church transfer document.' However this seems to have been an internally agreed regulation for the sake of good order rather than any binding obligation. During the next year Mr Edge's name was added to the list by mutual consent.

During the period of La Belle Époque in Dinard church attendance continued to increase, and such was the use of the church that it became necessary to make more permanent arrangements for the care, maintenance and cleaning. On 29th January 1892 the salaries of Mr and Mrs Clark were discussed. Mr Clark had been verger since the beginning, thus inaugurating the longest association with St Bartholomew's of any family. The terms of their employment were made clear in accordance with the best modern practice for job specifications that the:

Ornaments connected with the altar, lectern and so forth should be kept bright and in good order;

That the fire should be lit on all occasions necessary and also the gas (when required) as customary heretofore;

That the garden should be kept swept of all leaves as also the roof of the shed at the back of the church;

That Mr Clark should attend all Sunday services and not absent himself from any without special leave of the Chaplain. He will attend to the vestry being kept clean and in good order and see that good, fresh water is there supplied for use.

Mrs Clark guarantees to see the Church kept thoroughly clean, all rugs, cushions and properties belonging to members of the congregation returned after cleaning to their respective places.

Both Mr & Mrs Clark enjoined to take particular care in the storing of the altar cloths in the box appointed for that purpose.

A church which is cared for as the Clark family cared for St Bartholomew's over two whole generations is fortunate indeed, but this original job specification reveals how confident and strong was the growing congregation at the end of the nineteenth century.

At the same meeting the chaplain was congratulated on

the progress the church had made during his tenure and
was requested to record the Committee's pleasure in a
special book. Not wanting to miss an opportune moment.
the chaplain immediately asked the Committee's permission to purchase two more surplices, two vellum Prayer

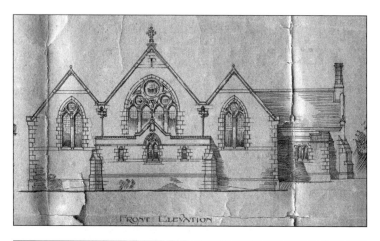

The plans and sketches above and on the following pages show details
of the proposed alterations to the interior and exterior, 1895–96 by
Charles Walker, Architect, of Newcastle-upon-Tyne.

SKETCH OF INTERNAL COLUMNS

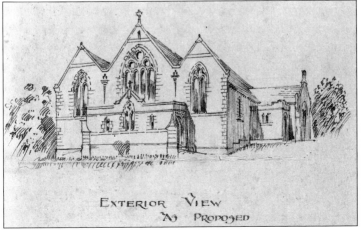

EXTERIOR VIEW
AS PROPOSED

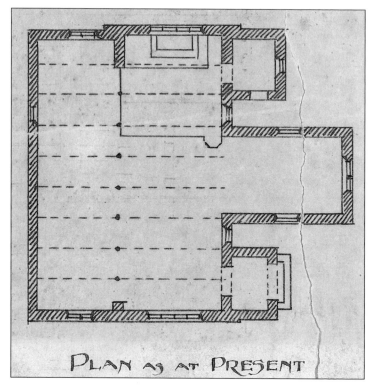

PLAN as at PRESENT

Books and a dozen hymn books with music, for the use of the choir whose only mention in the history of the church comes a month later when the hymn books have been presented to them by an anonymous donor. As far as we know, the local choir did not exist for long but years later, after the Second World War, St Bartholomew's became a popular venue for choirs from the United Kingdom. At this time the church was also carpeted throughout the 'church sittings' and designs for the reredos in place of the altar hanging were requested. This is still in place behind the altar.

All committees meet with strange requests from time to time, and in the same year, St Bartholomew's was approached by a Miss Young who requested permission to

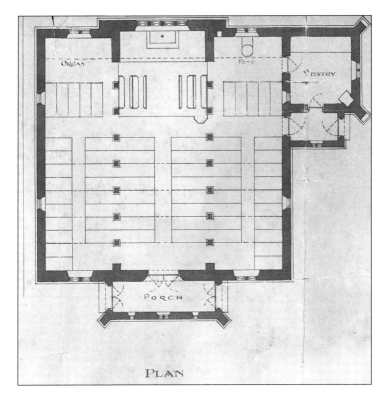

PLAN

use the water from the church cistern on a temporary basis. Alas the poor lady was refused in her hour of need as the committee wished to preserve their right of 'cutting off the connecting pipe at any time.'

The 'Trust' Debated

In September 1892, the committee were beginning to appreciate that new blood was required and there is a minute that the 'gentlemen named in the Trust viz: The Hon. Hercules Rowley, the Hon. Capt. Denison and Mr William Davy, consent to the appointment as Trustees, Sir Brian Egerton Bt. (in lieu of Sir Philip Egerton Decd.) Mr Spencer Chapman in place of Admiral Richard Wells, resigned, and

St Philip – a memorial window to Sir Philip Grey Egerton, one of the
main benefactors of the church.

in the event of their consents being obtained, that Mr
Herpin, notaire of St Malo be requested to prepare all the
necessary legal documents.'

Nothing seems to have come of this proposal which, in
any case was based on the misconception that they were
indeed a Trust, rather than owners of the freehold of the
property. There is no doubt of the Committee's awareness
that action needed to be taken to safeguard the future but
M. Herpin was in no position to initiate the change without
the property being sold. The matter was allowed to lapse
for ten years by which time the situation became desperate.

The Purchase of the Organ

Meanwhile the chaplain, Richard Peck, had been entrusted
with raising the money towards the purchase of an organ
in place of the harmonium. According to the records, the
Trustees, J. Forster, J. B. Carmac and George Marshall met
in the church on 6th February 1893 to 'decide upon the
best method of constructing the organ chamber having
ascertained that the Chaplain ... had a sufficient sum in
hand to admit of the commencement of the building.' Mr
Gervy, architect, was requested to draw up an estimate
which was subsequently approved. The surprising factor
about this is that the type and specification of the organ
was not considered until 17th July when Mr Peck presented
the committee, now joined by Sir George Duntze, with the
specification provided by Mr Alfred Oldknow of London.

After considerable discussion, which seems to have concentrated on the price and the contract rather than the
quality of the sound, the Committee agreed that it was
suitable for the church at a cost of 7000 Francs and asked
for it to be installed 'on or after 1st October 1893. Presumably by that time Mr Oldknow had to build an instrument
which would fit into the already constructed chamber, rather

than designing the chamber to fit the organ. However only two thirds of the cost of building the chamber [which was 3200 Francs] had been paid by that time, the remainder being retained for three months in case alterations and adjustments were needed so the arrangement was not totally bizarre. Before the final decision was made the Reverend Richard Peck and the organist of St Bartholomew's, Mrs Sortillo, went across to Dinan to hear the Great Organ in the Cathedral there, which had been built by Mr Oldknow. They pronounced the result satisfactory on 30th July and the final agreement was made with the organ builder.

At this time the church was showing a healthy surplus in its annual accounts and the raising of the 10,200 Francs for the organ and its chamber does not appear to have caused much difficulty. In fact the Committee were forced to borrow money from the organ fund in order to repair the church roof which was now found 'to be in an unsafe condition'. All this was done when the Hon. Secretary of the Committee was absent in Paris and St Bartholomew's is described for the first time in the minutes as 'the Anglican Church'.

By February 8th 1894, the organ was in full use but one further arrangement had to be made in order to ensure its efficiency in accompanying the services. On that day at a meeting in the Dinard Club the Chaplain proposed, seconded by Mr Edge, that 'Samuel Clark, the present Clerk of the Church be permitted to supply from his own family a boy to blow the bellows of the new organ at a salary of 25 Francs per quarter'.

During the last century or so it has been the custom for many churches to become cluttered with redundant and unnecessary musical instruments. St Bartholomew's managed to avoid this by a sensible arrangement with the new organist, Mr John Smith. He was loaned the harmonium 'upon the condition that it should be returned on the termination of his appointment, at his expense and should it be required at any time to replace the organ.' This arrangement continued happily during Mr Smith's time.

Finance in the 1890s

The church under Richard Peck and a highly organised and committed Committee was prospering. A surplus income of some 2000 Francs per annum was being raised but it was also recognised that it could rely on no outside help from any source other than its own voluntary contributions. The Committee minutes also recognise that the church officers consisted of 'Trustees', now seriously declining in number and becoming elderly and 'ordinary members'. To these was added the name of Sir Francis Blackwood.

In common with most parish churches in England, one means of raising a regular income was by means of pew rents. But while this was a convenient and acceptable means of income for the permanent residents, Dinard was in a special position on account of its large number of seasonal and casual visitors who were present for only a few weeks in the year and who had no wish to pay an annual pew rent. Subletting of pews was a practice which had turned into a scandal and strict new rules were introduced on 16th April 1894 to regulate the ownership of the sittings. These regulations illustrate the demand for seats and the society from which the congregation came:

> No pew holder, subletting his(or her) house shall have power or authority to sublet his (or her) sittings or bench during his (or her) absence from Dinard.

> That any person temporarily occupying as subtenant any house of which the owner or tenant is a pew-owner, shall have the preference given to him (or her) of taking over the bench or sittings belonging to his (or her) landlord upon

payment of the usual charge for sittings to the Church Committee for the period of his (or her) subtenancy,

That every householder possessing annual sittings, who may have arranged to leave Dinard temporarily shall give notice of the duration of his (or her) absence to the churchwarden, to enable him to sublet the sittings for such period and in order that they may be vacated by the date upon which the annual pew-renter shall return.

It was unanimously resolved that visitors who take sittings for six months in the Church of St Bartholomew, Dinard be accorded no advantage over those who take sittings for a shorter period and that the printed tariff of charges as posted with the church porch be resumed.

The new benches required for the new wing of the church, be arranged for and ordered by the Trustees in residence i.e. Messrs Marshall and Camac.

The final resolution may refer to the proposed extension suggested by Charles Walker, Architect, of Newcastle upon Tyne who had acted upon a request from Mr Camac. The latter was thanked for his work in 'connection with the enlargement of the church' but unless this was somehow included in the building of the organ chamber, it is difficult to see how it was enlarged, although the new benches were duly bought and placed in the North aisle. The amount of seating in church was extended at this time for the Trustees acknowledged a generous gift by Mr Mappin 'towards the Enlargement and Organ Fund'.

The chaplain had also been asked to find out how other continental churches managed their pew rents but after hearing from Pau, Paris and Rome, the Committee agreed that 'none of these cases exactly coincided with that of the Chaplaincy of St Bartholomew, Dinard and therefore afforded no data upon which the Committee could in any way act or proceed.'

The children's window, paid for by members of the Sunday School in
1895–96.

Pew rents continued to be a source of concern and there is no doubt that it became an issue for many members of the congregation until their abolition within living memory. The present writer well recalls his time as a curate in Great Grimsby when, although pews no longer had to be rented, many members of the congregation objected seriously when they found their own seat taken. One lady in 1894 was written to on account of her pew rental being so far in arrears that, if she did not pay up in full, 'the sittings would not be retained' for her and she would have to find a seat amongst the benches at the back. For the present a further modification of the rules concerning pew rental was proposed and seconded by Sir George Duntze and Sir Francis Blackwood that 'residents at Dinard, having freeholds on houses by the year, shall have power to hold their benches or sittings taken by the year absolutely and entirely at their control to dispose of as they may wish during their tenure providing they pay in advance the sum of fifty per cent over and above the tariff posted upon the Church Notice-Board, for such benches or sittings'.

In order to enforce the pew arrangements a 'regulation gown' was provided for the verger to emphasise his authority to remove people wrongly seated. During these times it required even more than usual courage for the casual worshipper to enter the church in order to worship!

The Completion of a Ministry and a Formative Period for the Church

Richard Peck's six years as chaplain of St Bartholomew's had been rewarding and successful. In 1895 he could rightly claim to have won the support of the majority of the congregation and the confidence of the Committee. He had conducted public Morning and Evening Prayer on every day of the week in accordance with the Book of Common Prayer and the Holy Communion was celebrated on Saints' Days and Sundays when numbers steadily increased with some 200 communicants at Easter and during the summer. The church finances were secure and there was even a Children's Church meeting regularly to which the window on the South wall of the church, next to the porch provides ample testimony, although it was erected after he had gone:

> This window is placed here to the glory of God by the English and American children attending the children's services 1896–7.

During Richard Peck's chaplaincy, the Right Reverend Richard Garnett, Bishop of Manchester, came to administer confirmation on Easter Day, 1892 as did the Bishop of Fulham, whose jurisdiction extended to North and Central Europe, two years later, with a large number of candidates. After this the Reverend E. D. Tibbits from the diocese of Albany, the first of many priests from the United States, officiated in St Bartholomew's on 21st July 1892. Peck himself may have attracted larger congregations than usual on account of the fact that he preached only on rare occasions, preferring to allow the service to speak for itself. After a successful and manifestly rewarding chaplaincy the Revd Richard Peck vacated the chaplaincy on 31st August 1895 to become rector of Bransteignton in Devon.

CHAPTER FIVE

Into the New Century

It is not known how many applicants there were for the vacant chaplaincy at St Bartholomew's, although it is evident that posts in the European chaplaincies were popular and sought after at this time. A few years earlier there had been thirty-four applicants for Dinan and there is no reason to suspect that Dinard was less popular. The choice of parson was taken very seriously as the minutes of the Church Committee show and on 18th January 1896, Mr Villiers Forbes, honorary secretary and churchwarden recorded the precise terms under which the new chaplain would be appointed. Writing to the Reverend Percy Carmichael Clarke he laid down the conditions of interview and appointment:

> ... in justice to the members of the congregation of the Church here, they [the members of the Committee] cannot depart from a long established Rule viz: That the candidates for a vacant chaplaincy shall officiate at least at one of the Church services and preach a sermon, prior to his election; and shall moreover guarantee to conduct the various services as hitherto carried on, i.e. in its present moderate tone as in vogue at Dinard, or what is usually understood as 'Cathedral Services'. The six months notice to be given to the chaplain would only be applied in the event of scandalous conduct or the introduction of 'Ritualistic practices' at variance with the wishes of the majority of the congregation.'

He was also promised removal expenses up to £20 or 500 Francs to move from Napton Vicarage near Rugby.

For his part, Mr Clarke offered to make only 'little alterations to details of Ritual' and to conduct the church services 'very decently, very reverently and very orderly' with 'this great aim in view of the spiritual advancement and welfare of those to whom I have the privilege to minister.' However he gave warning that he was not prepared to submit to everything that the Church Committee and laity wanted.

> You will of course, Gentlemen, understand that I have been brought up and educated in a certain school of thought and I cannot sacrifice principles, but in matters of ceremonial, without any deep spiritual truths involved, I attach but little importance or significance. I have never worn vestments nor used incense or heard confessions. I have always had lights at celebrations, Eastward position, mixed chalice, coloured stoles, ablutions etc. Beyond these reverent and decent acts of ritual I have not gone and moreover do not desire to go. I trust therefore that your Committee will place the utmost confidence in me and not check me in doing what I consider conducive to the well-ordering of the Church service and moreover what is quite in consonance with the teaching of the Prayer Book.

The service and sermon which Mr Clarke conducted took in Dinard 'gave every satisfaction' and he was duly appointed on a salary of 4000 Francs plus five offertories, which was one fewer than those enjoyed by his predecessor. In his letter of appointment, his contract was to last for no longer than three years.

Although this means of appointment had more in common with Free Church practice in England than established Anglican methods, it seems to have received the Bishop of London's rapid consent, for the permission to officiate was given as from 1st October 1895.

For family reasons the church organist Mr John Smith announced his resignation after two years' service for which the Committee commended him for the 'able and attendant manner in which he had performed his duties' and then wrote to the Reverend P. C. Clarke inviting him to find a successor. He soon wrote back to assure them that he had 'interviewed and obtained the services of a First Class organist on a salary of £50 and that she would reside with Mr Clarke, taking charge of his children when not occupied with her duties as organist.'

Purchase of the Parsonage Ground

Mr Clarke was soon to make his presence felt. At this time the chaplain was housed in a rented house belonging to a member of the congregation but, having held a parish and its freehold in England, the new chaplain wanted his own parsonage. Steps were taken to purchase the land adjacent to the church garden, belonging to Francois Lambol, Baron de Fougeres. The matter was complicated by the fact that he was legally separated from his wife, Marie Berthe Gros de Besplas, but under the terms of their contract of marriage, it was found that she had the right to sell. The Church Committee offered 16,000 Francs which was initially turned down but a satisfactory purchase was made and completed by 14th October 1896. At the time the church did not have sufficient funds for the purchase and the guarantors were Mr Marshall, Mr Forster and Colonel Forbes. The Revd P. C. Clarke also agreed to make a loan of £800 at 5 per cent per annum to the committee for the purchase and agreed that no building should be commenced until all the loans had been paid off. In the title deeds only Mr Marshall's and Mr Forster's names appear as owners and this, with the ownership of the church, was to cause recurring difficulties in the future. By the next year the church members were being asked to subscribe to the 'Parsonage Fund' in order to pay off the debt. One immediate outcome of the loan given by the Reverend Percival Clarke was that he requested that his tenure of office should be extended to five years from the original three and the Committee had little option but to accede to the request.

The church finances began to come under strain at this time for there appears to have been a falling off of pew rents due to smaller congregations, added to which the bank inadvertently paid the chaplain an extra 1000 Francs for the chaplain's salary. By 1898 the committee, which was becoming dangerously small, comprising only Mr Forster, Sir George Duntze and Colonel Forbes as regular resident members had decided that a parsonage was not a valid proposition and erected a board with a notice to sell although no price was agreed.

The impression is that relationships between the Committee and the parson had cooled very quickly after Percy Clarke's appointment, on account of his spending habits and ambitions as well as occasional bouts of absenteeism. Nevertheless he inaugurated the very first Midnight Communion service to be held on Christmas Eve 1896. There were 48 communicants which caused no reduction in the packed services the next morning. He was clearly an effective priest with a great deal of drive and initiative, for congregations were maintained and the children's services became very popular and numbers grew. A large confirmation was held by Bishop Wilkinson in the September of next year. But by 1897 it was necessary for the Committee to curtail the chaplain's spending habits and to rule that 'no payments excepting for bare necessities should be sanctioned'.

This was at the height of La Belle Époque but it coincided with new anxieties and disquiet at St Bartholomew's which began to look as if it might suffer the fate of the other local Anglican churches. In 1897 when Queen's Diamond Jubilee was duly celebrated with a well-attended service, there were increasing records that 'no services were held on account of the chaplain's illness' and in October the church was

closed 'for necessary Chancel painting.' Ill-health may have
been the underlying reason why Percy Clarke had originally
applied for the more temperate climate of Dinard for, by
1898 his condition was becoming serious and he had to
retire to England in the spring. It was also clear that, successful as he was, the strain of maintaining the church
numbers and frequent conflicts with members of the Committee were taking their toll. By appointing Mr Clarke as
chaplain, the Committee found they had put a race horse
in the shafts of a farm cart! Furthermore the weather in
Dinard during this year was 'persistently wet, very stormy
and boisterous' and by November it was described in the
parish register as 'very bad'.

The church minutes book records anxious meetings about
the debit balances each year and occasionally gives reasons.
By February 1900 Colonel Forbes was calling the attention
of the Committee (now only two others apart from himself)
to 'the fact that the Offertories during the season had declined owing to the unavoidable absence of the Chaplain,
and one of his substitutes, the Reverend Richard Granville,
as *locum tenens* 'not proving equal to the occasion.' He
suggested that in future, the name of the *locum tenens*
should be (as heretofore) submitted for the approval of
the Committee prior to confirmation by the Bishop, thus
releasing the chaplain from the responsibility of finding
one. It has been a characteristic of every Committee of
St Bartholomew's down to the present day, that the appointment of its chaplain should be a jealously guarded preserve
of the laity and on the whole it has worked well.

The church debt continued to cause concern to the end
of the century and beyond and the chaplain was urged to
organise a bazaar as well as circulate the congregation about
the need to liquidate the debt. But at the end of the year
the church was still in debt to the tune of 3255.10 Francs
and although the Bank agreed not to charge interest while

the congregation were engaged in collecting funds to pay off the debt, the accounts still showed a deficit of some 2736 Francs a year later.

Another set-back came when H. Villiers Forbes who had been honorary secretary for so long, decided that he had had enough, though he may also have been spending more time away from Dinard, and he resigned his position on 11th February 1901, writing as follows:

> Gentlemen,
> I have tendered my resignation before this, but in consequence of your request have withdrawn it. I have now to inform you that it is my resolve to cease from occupying the position of Honorary Secretary to the Church Committee from the 1st August next, thus affording you sufficient time to fill up my place.

Mr J. Forster took on the role of temporary Hon. Secretary as well as chairman and it was he who had the unenviable task of proposing on 25th February 1902, that the chaplain's salary should be cut to £140 per annum. Although there is no record in the minutes of the chaplain being present on this occasion, it is recorded that 'before this could be seconded the Chaplain expressed his acquiescence with the proposal.' By this time the salary was paid monthly in Francs and the new rate was to be 291.25, given that the exchange rate remained at around 25 Francs to the pound at this time. The unfortunate lady organist did not fare so well as her salary was to come from voluntary contributions from church members who may or may not have been satisfied with her performances. The minutes also mention the only recorded criticism of the Clark family during their long service at St Bartholomew's when it was decided to defer a decision about the verger's salary 'on account of the dissatisfaction expressed by the Chaplain about the way the church was being cleaned and looked after by the family.'

One wonders if this at least in part was the jaundiced outlook of a sick man.

What does become clear is that, even at this time as well as during the greater part of the century to come, the church depended for the most part of the generosity of visitors during the season. In view of this Mr Forster urged that 'every effort should be made during the coming season to ameliorate the condition of the finances, if not to entirely wipe out the present debt.' It was also hoped that the chaplain's salary should be restored to its former figure as soon as the finances were restored to a surer foundation.

In the midst of this gloomy period in the life of St Bartholomew's, Percy Clarke conducted his last service early on Easter Morning after which he fell ill and died soon after. He was buried in Dinard cemetery. The Bishop of North and Central Europe was immediately informed and a letter of appreciation of the chaplain's work sent to his brother. As a memorial to the chaplain and his work in St Bartholomew's, a handsome window was placed at the West End of the church 'by the English and American colony of Dinard to the glory of God and in affectionate remembrance of Percy Carmichael Clarke for seven years the chaplain, who entered into his rest on 13th April 1902. When I wake up after thy likeness I shall be satisfied with it.'

His widow expressed her thanks and gratitude to the church Committee 'for their kind expressions of sympathy and beg[ged] to assure them that it [was] a source of the greatest consolation to her in her hour of trial to receive such genuine evidence that her beloved husband was so completely appreciated'.

Whatever tensions and strains had been experienced between Percy Clarke and the Committee during these difficult years, these were soon forgotten in the recollection of his years of faithful work.

A Crisis of Vacancy and Management

Again there seems to have been no shortage of clergy wishing to do duty at St Bartholomew's at this time and the Reverend G. Harper was engaged as *locum tenens* during the summer season after the death of Mr Clarke. His remuneration was meagre for the Church Committee responded reluctantly to his request for a grant by offering one hundred francs for his services. He also applied for the chaplaincy but was informed on 11th August that 'the Committee desired to express their regret that they are unable to entertain your application.'

Another applicant, the Reverend Nesfield Andrewes, was approved and was settled in by the end of the year. There was some hesitation about his appointment, however, as he could only be made 'permanent' subject to the approval of the Lord Bishop of Northern and Central Europe, 'in the event of any complaint being preferred against him as a clergyman of the Church of England, or incapacity on account of age.' This is another indication, which comes up time and again, that the majority of clergy applying for posts in this part of Europe were either retired or suffering from ill-health. It was perceived that such a chaplaincy as Dinard might be less demanding than an English parish. Mr Andrewes was certainly content to receive a smaller stipend than his predecessor.

Mr Andrewes' tenure was brief and, although he conducted services for some months there is no record of his having received the bishop's permission. The Committee met again to discuss the question of the newly vacant chaplaincy on 9th January 1904 but decided to defer any decision as more pressing and serious matters were urged upon them about the position of the ownership of the Church and the Trusteeship.

The interest on Mr Clarke's loan for the parsonage was

due and had to be paid to the widow. John Forster paid this out of his own resources, and in order to ease the situation, he and Mr Marshall arranged to pay off the debt altogether, but at a charge to the church at the reduced rate of 4 per cent, payable half-yearly. Colonel R. V. Forbes rented the land at a sum of fifty francs per annum which left the committee to find some 650 francs each year for land which was proving useless to them.

The problems associated with the proposed parsonage reminded the Committee of the situation of the original church trustees who had purchased the church in 1884. Of the original eight who had signed as the new owners, seven were now dead and the more recently appointed members of the Committee were unaware of the legal situation. It was decided that a new chaplain could not be appointed until the Trusteeship and ownership of the church was settled. Mr Herpin, notaire of St Malo was consulted and his judgement awaited. The Committee were no doubt surprised to discover that the church was still in private ownership and the remaining owner, in French law, had the power to dispose of the church grounds and building as he wished. They were also shocked by the legal penalties they were required to pay for the loss of the previous trustees and owners. This had an effect on their decisions which was to cause further problems later on.

In view of the ownership question and the fragile nature of the terms of management by the Church Committee it is interesting that the real work of St Bartholomew's was continuing without interruption. Christmas and Easter communicants averaged between 80 and 170 and the regular round of services on Sundays were maintained at the times which were then universal throughout the Anglican Communion with an 8.0 a.m. Holy Communion, Matins at 11.00 and Evensong at 6.30 p.m. Attendances at Matins and Evensong varied between 24 and 60 people according to the season. Processions of Palms and other mildly catholic ceremonies took place at festivals, the children's services continued to be well attended and there was a regular series of concerts by visiting musicians which helped to entertain the residents and boost church funds.

Royalty occasionally attended the church during this time when Dinard had become a major fashionable resort for the British, and the Duke and Duchess of Connaught became regular worshippers, bringing their guests, among whom was Lord Salisbury's son. St Bartholomew's showed little sign of conforming to the habits and culture of its French hosts and remained a thoroughly British institution, observing Imperial and English national events in the manner of churches in Britain while ignoring French national events. Special services were held for Queen Victoria's Diamond Jubilee and again for her death on 22nd January 1901 and there was a great party for the celebration of King Edward VII's coronation after the service on 9th August. In spite of the ever-present financial anxiety special collections were sent to England for the relief of the poor in various parishes, particularly to St Clement's, Notting Hill and for overseas missions such as UMCA. The church was thriving and there was now a need for a long incumbency to stabilise the situation, to restore the organisation and to establish the atmosphere of a regular parish church to minister to the ex-patriot congregation and the summer residents. But the congregation would have to wait patiently through a period of crisis.

CHAPTER SIX

Crises During
La Belle Époque

The Committee, already burdened with the debts on the parsonage ground, the need for general repairs and a reduced income owing to the absence of a regular chaplain, found itself responsible for paying fines to the French authorities in respect of the deaths of the Trustees. The bill for this had been presented on 29th March 1904 after Mr Herpin's enquiry into the ownership of the church:

Sir Philip Egerton	215.88 Fr
Admiral the Hon. A Denison	258.50
William Davy	323.13
Col. The Hon. Hercules Rowley	430.65
Stamp Duty	.74
Total	1228.90

According to the treasurer's records there were further costs in addition to the notary's fees and the total bill amounted to some 4,500 Fr or nearly £200. This was to influence the Committee's decision about the future ownership which would again cause serious problems for the church.

Mr George Marshall, who had become the sole owner of the church owing to the death of the other trustees, could see no way forward apart from passing the ownership and trusteeship into the hands of the SPG, who were already responsible for the all the other churches in Brittany. He asked that the society should take over the church and that St Bartholomew's should appear on the list of Continental chaplaincies which the Society produced each year for the benefit of tourists. This list had been published for some thirty-five years yet there remained no mention of the Anglican church in Dinard.

His request was discussed at the Continental Chaplains Committee with the result that a letter was sent from them to Mr Marshall to the effect that 'the Society regrets that it has no funds unpledged and available for contributing to the transfer of the property [into the hand of the Society] but it would be prepared to advance £40 under pledge of repayment if that would make arrangements easier.' It also agreed to recommend that 'the Society should order its corporate Seal to be affixed to all documents necessary for vesting the church at Dinard and its site in the Society.' Thus the Society which had refused to countenance the support of an Anglican church in Dinard in 1870 'on account of the English population being too small to merit it' gave a further rebuff to the now flourishing community. Once again St Bartholomew's was made aware that it was on its own and would have to pay its own way and be responsible for its own affairs.

On 18th March 1904 the Committee, comprising Sir George Duntze, Captain Hody and Reginald Forbes met to consider George Marshall's proposition and the possibility of handing over the assets to SPG in view of their conditions. They wisely decided to have none of it and 'would endeavour to meet the debt incurred on the death of the Trustees'. Their decision was welcomed by members of the congregation and barely ten days later a letter was received from Lady Ada St Leger, widow of the general giving moral and material support:

Gentlemen,
    Having read Mr Herpin's statement regarding the debt on St Bartholomew's church, Dinard, I wish as a memorial to my late husband, to pay the amount required, one hundred

pounds, on the express condition that the church is not handed over to the SPG but that it is carried on as it has been before, in the hands of Trustees and Committee.

I am, Gentlemen

Yours faithfully,
Ada St Leger.

In addition there remains a very fine memorial tablet to her husband in the north aisle of the church.

During 1904 the task of appointing new Trustees, in French law, owners of the church, went ahead. There was always a danger that Mr Marshall, who had every right to dispose of the church and land on the open market, might do so, as he was now living in Canterbury and had no further interest in St Bartholomew's. However he agreed to a sale on the same conditions as that undertaken in 1884 and a new consortium of four persons was appointed.

In order to avoid the future payment of French taxes and fines through the death of the owners, two of the appointees were minors. These were E. B. Hody and Duncan Morison who were represented by their respective fathers along with Reginald Forbes and John Davy. The agreed price was 18,766 Francs 'consentie et acceptée directement entre elles, sans la participation en aucune sorte de Mr Herpin,' and probably reflecting the actual estimated value of the property.

The transfer was made and the Deeds signed on the 1st December 1904.

The Search for a Chaplain

Meanwhile, the Committee felt justified in seeking a new and permanent chaplain. The Reverend E. Harper was acting as *locum tenens* once again but had to press the committee for recompense 'for the services he had rendered to the chaplaincy in emergencies.' There was never any consideration of his being appointed a full-time chaplain but an application from a Reverend George Crawford looked promising. He was invited to come over to Dinard in order to preach and minister at the Sunday services but on further enquiries he declined 'on account of the stipend being insufficient and the restriction as to the necessity of the chaplain remaining in office during the season being too inconvenient for himself and his family.'

The post was advertised and several applications were received. In line more with nonconformist tradition than Anglican, two clergymen were invited to Dinard in the July to take services while the long-suffering Mr Harper was again asked to be *locum tenens* during the summer. By 21st October the committee had found a firm applicant whom they elected unanimously. The Reverend F. E. Freese was asked to receive permission from the Bishop of London to officiate in Dinard and was appointed to the chaplaincy from 1st December subject to the conditions that his tenure was for five years and he was to give six months' notice if he desired to leave. The Committee for their part, also agreed to give six months' notice 'in the event of conduct unbecoming a clergyman, or such conduct as to lead the congregation to withhold their support in aid of the chaplaincy, or in the event of such bad health as to incapacitate him from the performance of his duties.' In particular the Committee insisted that the chaplain should make a point of officiating during the season from 15th July to 30th September. Past experience had strengthened the conditions imposed.

Very soon St Bartholomew's became responsible for providing the services and looking after the churches at St Enogat and St Lunaire where Mr Harper remained to officiate during the season. The Bishop of London wrote to the Committee suggesting that the 'services of the Church'

should be held in both resorts during the season and that
the chaplain at Dinard should find 'desirable' clergymen to
officiate. A piece of land was promised by a Mr Laraque for
the erection of a chapel of ease which, it was proposed,
should be secured in *propria firma* and funds for building
the chapel should be raised. One of the reasons for this was
that, in spite of the management problems and the delay
in the appointment of the chaplain, St Bartholomew's congregation had grown larger than ever. Plans for the
enlargement of the building were again discussed as Easter
communicants were now in excess of 200, as was the
regular congregation during the summer months. However
the church debt, still amounting to 18319.54 Francs in 1905,
prevented any reconstruction although new doors were
placed in the church porch and the cistern and pump were
given attention.

The Committee under the newly appointed chairman, Sir
George Duntze, continued to meet regularly and to take
their duties very seriously during this period. On 29th May
1905, following a request from Mr Freese that the chaplain
should be able to appoint his own churchwarden, the Committee proposed that 'two churchwardens should be elected
at the Easter Vestry meeting each year.' They were instructed
to 'consult together on every matter affecting the management of the church expenditure i.e., not exceeding in
amount the ordinary expenditure of the church.' The
'People's Warden' was also instructed to send written notice
to every member of the congregation notice of the Vestry
meeting stating the agenda. Rules for the conduct of meetings were also laid down. Sixteen years before the
establishment of Parochial Church Councils in the parish
churches of England, Dinard was setting up a management
arrangement which anticipated their introduction.

The Reverend F. E. Freese was not one to allow events to
take their course and was very active in his attempt to resolve

outstanding matters. The Parsonage Ground was a contin-
ual worry and the problem of raising money for the building
of St Lunaire church may have been shelved but for his
persistence. During his time he seems to have been the
effective chairman of the Committee and clearly put pressure on the Reverend E. Harper to present plans for the
financing and building of the church. The story of St Lunaire church has already been told, but it is significant that
the Bishop of North and Central Europe as well as SPG were
quite happy for the Trustees and Committee of St Bartholomew's to become effective 'patrons' of the church and act
as security for the funds. SPG admitted they had neither
the funds nor the inclination to support the erection of the
chapel of ease in spite of the recommendation by the Bishop
or North and Central Europe. The ground was conveyed
into the ownership of the committee of Dinard church.

At St Bartholomew's the Committee decided to renew the
church heating 'as the chaplain had objected to the burning
of coke in the church stove on account of the fumes of
sulphur issuing from it.' The churchwardens decided to try
anthracite instead and employed the local contractor
M. Brossard to install the new equipment at a cost of around
18,000 Francs.

Another minute concerns the request of a Colonel Davidson who asked permission to play on the church organ
but the Committee refused on the grounds that it established a precedent and that the organ was reserved for pupils
and for those practising for the services.

Under the chaplaincy of Mr Freese questions of churchmanship were occasionally raised because he was rather
more inclined to the ritualism which made some of the
congregation uneasy. The particular case brought before the
Committee was 'the use of candles at funerals, lately introduced'. The Committee agreed in the case of one funeral
but voted unanimously 'with the assent of the chaplain' that

the 'use of candles around the coffin should be disconti-
nued.' Another example of the chaplain's inclination to take
decisions without consultation was over the employment of
the gardener and organ blower, Mr Clark, with whom he
agreed that he should work until 12 noon on specified days
instead of Wednesdays and Fridays. The arrangement only
came to the Committee's notice when the organ blower
failed to turn up for a Friday evening choir practice.

But more was to come, and the end of Mr Freese's
chaplaincy was not a happy one. The uneasy relationship
between this obviously dominant chaplain and the highly
capable Committee was finally destroyed when the Honorary Secretary received a note from Mr Freese informing the
Committee that he 'had appointed Mr Harper to perform
the duties of *locum tenens* during the month of October in
consequence of his proposed absence for the purpose of
assuming his duties, on his appointment to the Chaplaincy
of Wiesbaden'.

An emergency meeting was called and the chaplain was
asked to continue his work in Dinard until the expiry of his
term on 31st October 1906. Unhappy as they were with Mr
Freese, they obviously preferred him to poor Mr Harper
who was always ready to take on whatever was asked of
him. However they expressed their intention to appoint their
own *locum tenens*.

The chaplain was furious. He replied saying that he refused to regard the authority of the Committee in the
absence of Captain Hody and Colonel Ponsonby and declined to consult them in the matter of the appointment of
the *locum tenens*. Moreover he claimed the sole right to be
chairman of the Committee in his position as chaplain 'at
any meeting convened.'

Alas, although the minutes of the Committee record that
the correspondence was being 'kept for reference', the letters
detailing the accusations cannot be found but there is no

doubt that face to face meetings were no longer possible and that the final outcome was acrimonious. The Committee wrote to the chaplain informing him that 'he ceased to be a member of the Committee on resigning the chaplaincy and his presence was not required in the selection of the next chaplain or of the *locum tenens* – and further that his attack on a member of the Committee was considered unjustifiable and his statements so exaggerated they must decline to discuss them.'

A letter from Mr Freese, dated 31st August 1906, was received by the committee as follows:

I have just seen Mr Harper and as a result of our interview, have decided to ask the Bishop's permission to resign this chaplaincy on September 30th instead of October 31st. In the absence of the other members of the Committee, and in view of what has taken place, I do not feel inclined to accept responsibility for anything that might occur when I am no longer on the spot. As Chairman of the Committee, I desire to place on record my entire disapproval of the attempt to make that body responsible for the discourteous and irregular proceedings which you have undertaken in their name.

I am dear Sir

Yours faithfully F. E. Freese
Chairman of the Church Committee.

In reply the Committee reminded Mr Freese of his terms of appointment and the fact that it was the Committee which had appointed him as well as the fact that they had increased his salary and the number of offertories he received. They 'abstained from further reference to the title of Chairman to which they do not consider him to be entitled.' The church which had always been managed by laymen was to continue under their control. Their final letter on 1st September was:

In reply to your note of yesterday's date the Church

Committee was pleased to accept your resignation from 30th September seeing your appointment to Wiesbaden is announced for 1st October 1906.

The lack of courtesy on your part towards the church committee throughout your tenancy of this chaplaincy has been remarkable. Your attacks on the Hon. Secretary who has been the one of all others to study your interests, they consider unjustifiable and your accusation the result of a hasty conclusion unsupported by facts. The Committee hold themselves responsible for their proceedings which they are persuaded will meet with the approval of the two absent members.

We are, dear Sir,

> Yours most faithfully,
> H. Villiers Forbes Hon. Sec
> R. Villiers Forbes
> George Duntze Members

Although relations had broken down so completely between chaplain and Committee, it is only fair to note that F. E. Freese had made an important impact on the large congregation at Dinard when other local Anglican churches were beginning a serious and terminal decline. The children's services had reached their greatest numbers, the Bishop held regular confirmations and church membership remained very large. He also ensured that the problems the church faced were being addressed, although he did not remain long enough to see the biggest issues to a conclusion. It was the case of a very dominant priest failing to get on with a Committee of men used to command and being involved in all decisions.

In the ensuing emergency the Committee decided that the chairman should be elected alphabetically for each year with the result that Sir George Duntze remained as chairman for the ensuing year. The Reverend E. Harper was appointed *locum tenens* in the absence of anyone else at such short notice (at a salary of 75 Francs per week) and the Reverend Valpy French was appointed chaplain but only for a period of twelve months.

The Parsonage Ground

Much of 1905 to 1907 was taken up with the question of payments and ownership of the ground in front of the church which had been planned for the parsonage. The Committee had been under the impression that the land was mortgaged and that the payments were in respect of the mortgaged property. However Sir Francis Forster pointed out to the Committee's surprise and annoyance, that George Marshall and John Forster, Frank's brother, held the land on their own freehold and that the payments by the church committee were for the rent of the land. As an executor of his brother's will, he offered to sell that land to the church at the price that was paid for it. He also offered to subscribe £25 along with another £25 from his brother Charles 'on condition that the purchase is completed by August 30th 1906'. He said that Marshall was willing to give £5 on the same condition, failing which they would sell the land on the open market.

When the Committee looked into the question of owner-ship it was found that what they had thought had been a loan to the Reverend P. C. Clarke had in fact been a purchase made through M. Herpin the notaire who, on being con-sulted, considered that under French law Mr Marshall was the sole owner:

> J'ai l'honneur de vous faire savoir que le terrain situé devant l'Eglise Anglicane appartenait indivisement à M. Marshall et John Forster avec droit d'accroissement entre eux. Par suite du décés de ce dernier, le terrain appartient actuallement à Mr Marshall seul.

The Committee decided to consult the congregation about

the desirability of purchasing and retaining the land and, following a discussion, appointed a group of ladies to assist the Committee in raising the funds. It had been felt that to lose the land would mean to lose the tranquillity of the area surrounding the church. Thus we have the first mention of lady members of the church actively engaged in church work at St Bartholomew's – Mrs Ponsonby, Mrs Colquhoun, Mrs Hamilton, Mrs Villiers Forbes, Mrs Hughes and the chaplain's wife, Mrs Freese.

At this stage the Committee still thought they could negotiate a deal with Sir Frank Forster and made an offer which Sir Frank refused, irrespective of the fact that he no longer had an interest in the matter. Eventually the Committee wrote to him that they resigned all claim to the land and that he could do what he liked with it; this at a time when it had been proved that Mr Marshall was the sole owner. The matter lay dormant for some time until 1909 when the syndicate who owned the fabric of the church (Messrs Forbes, Hody, Davy and Morison) brought the land for 15,000 Francs of which 6000 came from church funds and 9000 Francs from Mr Forbes. A later impression was that the money was lent on a mortgage but no interest was ever paid nor was any part of the capital repaid.

The purchase of the land between the church and the road which had been intended for the parsonage, ensured the peace and tranquillity of St Bartholomew's. Although it was to lie fairly derelict and unused for another seventy years, the whole issue had alerted the Church Committee to the status of Anglican land and property in French law. Colonel Forbes, at the Committee's request, went to see the Mayor of Dinard once again who passed him on to the Bureau d'Enregistrement where it was explained that while the French Protestant Community was subject to French law under which their places of worship were given protection, the Anglican churches enjoyed no such benefit and were thus subject to the same regulations as private citizens and businesses. As a result, although the owners of the land and church property regarded themselves as holding the material assets in trust on behalf of the worshipping congregation, they had a legal right to sell the whole property if they chose to do so. The members of the church management committee who were not named owners had no power to prevent this. Clearly more secure arrangements needed to be made for the future of the church to safeguard the interests of the congregation but this was to be delayed for another two decades while St Bartholomew's enjoyed a period of peaceful tranquillity at a time when the rest of Europe was in turmoil.

CHAPTER SEVEN

A Long Chaplaincy and Peace in Time of War

Assurance of more peaceful times ahead came with the appointment of the Reverend Herbert Mills to the chaplaincy when the Reverend Valpy French confirmed that he did not wish to extend his twelve month appointment. Mr Mills, who had been a vicar in Torquay, was offered £160 *per annum* plus the offertories for five Sundays each year. As was the customary practice his letter of appointment stated the usual conditions that six months' notice of departure was to be given on either side although he could be dismissed instantly in the event of conduct unbecoming to a clergyman, debt or ill health. Another reason for dismissal was 'the introduction of ritual practices at variance with the wishes of the majority of the congregation'. This was a modification of the previous conditions which stated the precise details of the rituals objected to.

The Committee need not have worried. Herbert Mills proved to be a moderate Anglican, faithfully leading the daily offices and a full round of Sunday services without embellishment or innovation. As far as can be seen, he always consulted the Committee about any changes and during his long period of service by Dinard standards, he was never involved in any major controversy. His tenure of sixteen years was the longest service given by a full-time chaplain.

The congregation must have welcomed this eirenic priest with a sense of relief after the turbulent and energetic

The Matthew, Mark and Luke windows bought in 1909 from the redundant Anglican church of St Peter's Avranches, for £10.

époques of the Reverends Clarke and Freese and in antici-
pation of less anxious times following his arrival, Mrs Pratt
donated a new altar cloth and Mrs Cuthbertson new pulpit
covers. Mr Hamilton painted and redecorated the interior
of the church at his own expense and the parsonage ground
debts were soon to be paid off. Excess furniture including
a font, a processional cross, a lectern and a bookstand were
loaned to the newly built church at St Lunaire. This came
at a time when other Anglican churches in the area were
closing for lack of support and use and St Bartholomew's
benefited from the purchase of the four 'Evangelists' stained
glass windows from St. Peter's church, Avranches for £10
by an anonymous member of the congregation. These were
installed on the North wall of the church where they remain
to this day. By 1913 new electric lights had been installed.
Confidence and a sense of purpose were the hallmarks of
this period when all around the old ways were beginning
to collapse.

Money-raising efforts now followed the traditional pattern
of English parish churches with annual fêtes and a number
of concerts during the season which raised sufficient income to supplement the shortfall of funds caused by the
impending World War and the return of British and American families to their homelands.

Among those returning to England was Mr Clark, the
able and long-serving verger who had served the church so
well for the previous twenty years or so. In September 1913
the chaplain was requested to interview Mr Johnny Clark,
his son, for the post. Johnny had begun his service at St
Bartholomew's in 1894 as 'organ-blower' for the newly installed organ and he was seen to be the natural and
admirable choice to take over his father's post at a salary
of 125 Francs per month.

Episcopal Visitations

The Bishop's book of this time records two visitations made by Bishop Herbert Bury of North and Central Europe which suggests that Anglican bishops were much more active in making regular personal contact with their parishes than is the case today. On 23rd January 1912 the bishop arrived in Rennes from Bordeaux and was met by the Reverend H. B. Mills whom he questioned about his work. 'A large and friendly gathering' welcomed him at the Hotel Windsor on the next afternoon after which he paid a number of calls and entertained another large gathering at dinner in the evening. He also attended the daily services and celebrated the Eucharist at St Bartholomew's before going on to the chaplaincies across the River Rance at St Malo and Parame. Back to Dinard via Dinan he recorded that his visitation was 'an encouraging and pleasant one' before taking the boat back to England from Le Havre.

A second visitation took place in February 1914 when the bishop stayed with Mrs Cuthbert, his host on the previous occasion, having crossed the Rance by the vedette. He conducted a Confirmation in St Bartholomew's – 'a most beautiful and reverent service full of the spirit of prayer' which was followed by a great reception in the Hotel Windsor 'where there were maids and chauffeurs as well as their Masters and Mistresses at which I gave an address.' He stayed until the Sunday when he took the early Celebration at which 'there were 20 ladies present but not one man' and then preached at the 11.0 a.m. service to a 'large and attentive congregation.' During his visit he had lunch with Mrs Kitchener, mother of the Field Marshall, but did not neglect to spend time with Mr Mills about his work in the chaplaincy.

Contacts with the diocese were regular and cordial during Mr Mills' years and the bishop's advice was sought on several occasions. An intriguing request was made in 1910 when a group of Protestants sought permission to hold services in St Bartholomew's on Sundays between the Anglican services from 9.15 to 10.15. The bishop's reply was uncompromising:

Bradford Court,
Nr Taunton
14th July 1910

Dear Sir,

I have your letter of 12th. The church at Dinard is consecrated.

By the deed of consecration which is a legal instrument, a church is by that legal act, set apart for ever 'for the services of the Church of England and no other'.

This is the reply I always give to such requests as that now made to you. It furnishes us with a reason which cannot give offence.

Were the Dinard church not consecrated it is in my opinion, undesirable to share our churches with other bodies. It gives occasion to the Romans – who are not slow to use it as a taunt – that we are one of the many Protestant sects which so unhappily divide Christendom.

Yours ever,

H. Wilkinson
Bishop of North & Central Europe.

In fact the bishop was wrong in supposing that St Bartholomew's was consecrated but there is little doubt that it had been duly dedicated. There is an important but subtle difference between the two acts which lay people might consider typical of those brought up in the niceties of arcane theology. Consecration of a church may be performed only by a bishop and is designed for buildings expressly reserved for ecclesiastical use. Dedication of a church may be performed by a priest and is designed for temporary buildings perhaps built of wood or when it is intended to replace the building at some future time. The fact that the Bishop Bury (or Bishop of Derry?) only dedicated the church in 1879 may have been on account of its remaining in private ownership, thus creating some doubt about its future. But of greater interest is the bishop's reasoning that non-Anglican services in the church at the particular time might give offence to otherwise liberal-minded churchmen. He was probably correct.

The Great War

During the Great War congregations naturally diminished as families returned to the United Kingdom and families no longer came to spend the season in Dinard. The town and church however do not appear to have been unduly affected by the war and congregations remained fairly high. The registers show that the chaplain continued to preach on the great themes of the Christian year without undue emphasis on the war which must have been a constant theme of conversation and a source of anxiety for anxious relatives of those engaged in the fighting. Numbers were undoubtedly maintained by the remaining American population who remained neutral until towards the end of hostilities and communicant numbers remained between 49 at Christmas 1914, dropping to 35 at Easter 1917. Some British soldiers and sailors were buried in the cemetery including one Charles Nungessen who must have been one of the first 'aviators'. Otherwise the church registers make no further reference to that most devastating conflict.

The Last Days of Herbert Mills

Those families who had left Dinard during the war soon returned after 1918 and summer residents were greater than ever. No doubt there was a hope to resume the glamorous and decorous life of La Belle Époque in Edwardian time and a desire to create a new sense of peace away from the gloomy horrors and misery of the post-war years and the terrible influenza epidemic. This spread through Northern France and Great Britain, and, according to some commentators, took more lives than the Great War itself. Bishop Bury made three visitations in quick succession, in January 1920, in February 1922 in Mr Mills' final year and again in July 1924. On the first two occasions he stayed with Mrs Cuthbert thus continuing an arrangement which he had begun before the war but complained that the church Visitation book had not been produced for him, 'having been forgotten or overlooked during the war'. No mention is made of any discussions with the chaplain who must have been suffering from poor health during his visits. The bishop does however mention the excellence of the large receptions held in the Hotel Windsor and the large congregations at Evensong when he preached. His final visit, was his first during the summer, by which time the Reverend J. M. Vallance was chaplain, General and Mrs Smith-Dorrien, whose memorial plates are on the church wall, were his hosts. During it the bishop recorded how beautiful Dinard was looking and that the church and garden were 'all in beautiful order, the latter quite a glory of Rambler roses'. A tribute indeed to the work of the 'new' verger Johnny Clark.

As well as keeping in close contact with the bishop and diocese, Herbert Mills was a regular participant at the conferences which came to be held in the jurisdiction of North and Central Europe. Alas, however he does not seem to have been a great writer or communicator for nothing remains of his letters, addresses or notes to give us any clues about his day to day work apart from his meticulous keeping of the service registers from which we can judge that he was a caring and diligent priest. On his last Easter Day in Dinard a very nearly record number of 258 communicants were recorded.

Herbert Mills' last days in office were dominated by ill-health and he had to return to his wife's native Cardiganshire to seek to recover his health. The Church Committee were tolerant of his absence and he was given six months in which to recover while temporary locums were sought. Correspondence with Mrs Mills shows that his stipend was desperately needed as they had few if any other financial resources. This was a common problem for clergy without private means at this time as the Church paid no pensions. But the continuing payments to the chaplain as well as the cost of hiring locums proved too expensive and at the end of the six months General Richardson and Colonel Cameron of Lochiel wrote that 'it was most difficult to maintain the services of the church in a satisfactory state with chaplains changing every month.' Little did they know of what would be in store within thirty years! It was decided that the 334 francs and five collections paid to Mr Mills should cease from 1st January 1924. It was thus a mercy that he died on 12th July 1923. A fitting memorial plaque to this quiet, diligent and peace-loving priest is to be found above the vestry door in St Bartholomew's with the brief caption 'Simple service simply done'.

CHAPTER EIGHT

Between the Wars: the Constitution Revised

The arrival of the new chaplain, the Reverend J. M. Vallance, in Dinard coincided with a new influx of British citizens and the return of the old seasonal visitors who were determined to relive the carefree life of La Belle Époque. The comfortably-off found in Dinard a kind climate away from the grim drudgery of post-war England with its threats of turbulence and impending General Strike, and those who could afford it rented houses for the whole summer season. Mothers and daughters remained in Dinard while their husbands were absent on business in Britain or the Colonies earning the money and the boys were sent to suitable boarding schools. The influential majority came from military or colonial service families as the memorial plaques inside the church amply testify; and the chosen schools reflect this tradition as the majority of sons went on to Sherborne, Cheltenham, Wellington and Haileybury while a few of the most able or influential found places in Winchester, Eton or Harrow. The daughters usually stayed with mother and the maid and attended Dame Schools like Miss Cooke's in the present Boulevard Le Feart.

These days are recalled in a romantic novel by Mary Wesley and the scene is one in which the gentle climate, the freedom of the women, the coffee mornings, the beach parties, the casinos and the hotel dances in the long evenings were apt to lead to courtly flirtations and heart-tugging romances, especially when the boys came home from school or university. The mother of an old friend told me of her early life in Dinard where she attended the Dame School. It was at the dancing classes at the Hotel Crystal under a strict instructress, a Russian émigré, Madame Glinke where she remembers first meeting Miss Elizabeth Hannay. Mrs Margaret Walters, née Cooke, now retired to Trallong near Brecon recalls those days with the greatest affection, including the sometimes literally painful piano lessons with Mlle. Betti Prelle and the compulsory attendance at St Bartholomew's. The regular round of social life included church attendance, and St Bartholomew's benefited from the regular worship and generosity of the many generous residents and visitors. Amongst these was one of the leading ladies of the day, Mrs Hughes-Hallett, popularly known as the Queen of Dinard, who was well-known for her lavish entertainment and hospitality. She left a substantial legacy to the church on her death in 1922.

Amongst the newcomers in the twenties was Sir George Curtis who had married Monica Forbes, a daughter of the family who were such supporters of St Bartholomew's for many years. He had recently retired from a senior judicial post in colonial India. He and his wife were to play leading parts in the governance and maintenance of the church for years to come and their son, Geoffrey who had become a monk of the Community of the Resurrection in Mirfield, was to help the church out when no one else was available. It was Sir George Curtis who worked out a solution to the complicated and delicate business of the church ownership while most of the large and prosperous congregation remained quite unaware of the threat to the church which was still in private ownership under French law.

The Resolution of the Ownership Crisis

As a new member of the Committee Sir George undertook

the task of discovering the exact relationship between the church, the diocese, the Bishop of London and the congregation. As in 1904 he found that the Church Committee had long regarded themselves as Trustees on behalf of the congregation but that there was nothing in the Trust Deeds which justified that conception. Nor in French law were there any conditions regarding the usage to which the 'church' might be put. Indeed the very word 'church' was a misnoma as the Bishop of London had no powers of control except by courtesy of the owners who, fortunately, had always sought an acceptable chaplain who held the bishop's permission to officiate. St Bartholomew's had no legal standing except as a private dwelling and was used as a place of worship only by consent of the owners who might decide that it should not remain Anglican or even a church.

In 1919 E. B. Hody had died which left only three co-proprietors, Messrs Forbes, Davy and Morison, the latter two being minors at the time of the purchase in 1904. Mr Forbes resided in Dinard for five months of the year while the other two were entirely non-resident and had never taken part in the management of the church. They had been appointed as minors in the first place to avoid the necessity of paying fines should they die. It was found that Mr Morison had emigrated to British Columbia and, according to his step-mother, was not aware that he was a Trustee or co-owner of the church. Mr Davy had settled in London and never came near Dinard. Thus all the power and authority over the church was in practice concentrated in one person who was absent from Dinard for seven months in the year.

The serious danger for the church was that there was absolutely no guarantee that Morison or Davy would be willing to hand the church over without demanding a proper price for it. They might be hard pressed for money as so many of the former Edwardian middle classes were at this time. The Church Committee might thus find itself under attachment for the debts of the proprietors. Under the current circumstances the only way a legal enactment could be carried through would be for an order to be signed in London and counter-signed in British Columbia.

Furthermore, if all three of the remaining owners died, the whole property together with cash balances and the Parsonage Fund account would pass into the hands of the heirs of the one who died last. According to the Napoleonic Code this would almost certainly result in the church being sold and the Parsonage Fund being liable to English Estate duty.

Four possible solutions were presented by Sir George Curtis for the consideration of the Committee.

The first was that the church might be transferred to SPG or the Colonial and Continental Church Society. They would still have to negotiate with the owners and it would mean that the Committee in Dinard would no longer have the right of patronage to appoint their own priest. Sir George pointed out that every church in France, Le Havre excluded, had affiliated itself to one society or another and that, in his experience it was becoming harder to find competent priests without help from a society. He also reminded the committee that this was first proposed by George Marshall in 1904.

Secondly Sir George suggested that the present system of ownership might be continued by adding more names to the list. In fact this solution was discovered to be impossible in French law as it affected the 'inalienable rights of the legal proprietors' and would make the church a 'tontine', a legal arrangement which was then being suppressed. Also the arrangement would involve constant expenditure as fines would be payable on the decease of each proprietor. Finally it would simply delay the problem to some future date.

A third possibility was to convert the church into a limited liability company by forming a 'Société Anonyme' with a working capital of, say 40,000 Francs. The Society could take over the church land and assets for a nominal price and then lease it to an Association who would take over the running of the church. There could then be a controlling body, half of whom would be elected by subscribers of 100 Francs a year and half by benefactors who had contributed 1000 Francs to the church. The Association would pay the Society a rent of 2000 Francs per annum to make the statutory allocation to the reserves and the fixed tax. The advantage of all this would be in keeping with French law and encouraging the interest and support of the congregation by ensuring administration by those on the spot.

There was a fourth option to form a 'Société Culturelle' with the help of the British Embassy but the government of the day under M. Herriot was committed to the abolition of such groups and no consideration was given to this proposal.

The urgency of the situation became clearly recognised when the Hotel Roche Corneille next to the church began to make extensive alterations and it was feared that the interests of St Bartholomew's could not be defended because there was no one legally qualified to negotiate on behalf of the church, since there was no legal owner available. Consultations with other Anglican churches in France were carried out with the help of the Foreign Office and Embassy officials but there was no parallel case found which could be used to solve the problem. It was therefore left to the church's lawyer in St Malo to draw up a set of model statutes to fit the local conditions in Dinard. M. LeMasson recommended that an 'Association Cultuelle' should be created on the lines already used by Roman Catholic churches in France which allowed them to escape from tax obligations. This meant that a Managing Committee should be formed with a President and a body of benefactors and annual members. Sir George Curtis had already taken steps to create a committee formed by elected church members and the formation of the Association would not be difficult provided that the proprietors could be persuaded to hand over the property.

Mr Reggie Forbes carried out the negotiations with the absentee owners and the situation was satisfactorily resolved on the 28th June 1928 when the church was sold to the Association de L'Eglise Anglicane de Dinard for 100,000 Francs. For the first time since its erection, St Bartholomew's was officially recognised as a properly constituted place of worship and was described in legal documents as a 'church'. The managing committee's responsibility was 'the upkeep and improvement of the Anglican Church at Dinard and the appointment, on condition that the nominee is approved by the Bishop of London, of a chaplain duly licensed and the provision of funds for the holding of services according to the tenets of the Church of England.' One of the immediate plans of the committee was to consider once again the building of a parsonage for the use of the chaplain. The new Association meant that it was now possible to raise funds for church maintenance and development legally without risking their being confiscated by the French authorities or the church proprietors.

When these statutes came to be modified in 1951, it was thought that the church had been renamed as the British American or Anglo-American Church in Dinard but in the original statutes in French drawn up by M. LeMasson no such description appears. The description must have been an informal one to ensure that American residents had the right of full participation on the Church Committee and that priests from the Protestant Episcopal Church of the USA could be appointed as chaplains. This has given rise to a great deal of misunderstanding down to the present time and was the cause of the 'semi-detached' state of the church within the diocese of Europe. Some church members felt that St Bartholomew's ought to remain outside what became the Diocese in Europe so that it could feel equally a part of the American Episcopal Jurisdiction.

Another difficulty affecting its full status was the fact that membership of St Bartholomew's depended on the financial contributions to the church and that voting members must have paid their subscriptions. This is quite against the practice and principles of the Anglican Communion and therefore unacceptable to the diocese. It has always been the case that there is no official definition of membership of the Anglican Church and Communion apart from being baptised. Hopefully these anomalies are being finally put to rest in the new century and millennium.

The American Dimension

It is perhaps helpful to mention the peculiar status of the Anglican Communion in Europe and the dual relationship which the committee of St Bartholomew's sought to retain with both the American and English jurisdictions.

As far back as the 18th March 1867 the Continental Chaplaincies Committee received a letter from the Bishop of Pennsylvania informing them and the Bishop of London that Episcopalian services were to be held in Paris for the benefit of American residents. On 15th April of that year the Committee agreed that the American bishop should have the responsibility of providing clergy for the American congregations in Europe. Following a great deal of correspondence between the committee in London and the responsible bishop in the USA, the Bishop of Illinois asked the SPG for financial assistance for the growing number of American chaplaincies but SPG decided that they could not afford to share that burden. The Americans would have to look after themselves, and thus twin dioceses and twin administrations were created in Europe representing the same Communion and using the same language and Prayer Book.

The particular significance for Dinard was that the church had been built and maintained without any financial assistance from England and it was recognised that a large number of contributors to the church came from the American community. There was a natural desire to be recognised as a joint national church with access to the two bishops responsible for the Anglican community in Europe. In later years St Bartholomew's has had every reason to be grateful for its close connections with the American jurisdiction, not only for financial support but also in the provision of locum chaplains and indeed, its very survival during and after the Second World War.

Parish Routine and the British Cemetery

Amidst the continuing discussions and plans to create a system of management which would safeguard the future of the church and meet the needs of the congregation, normal 'parish' routine continued in much the same way as in parish churches in England. Apart from the usual pastoral work, the constant care of the sick amongst an aging population, the now declining children's work and the regular services, there was the constant demand for money-raising efforts, church repair and maintenance and larger projects. In all this Mr Vallance was clearly a respected chaplain and when he came to leave, having agreed to exchange 'livings' on the recommendation of the Bishop of London with the Reverend Frank Pickford, his departure was much regretted. A Dinard correspondent wrote in the Anglican Church Magazine, the magazine for North and Central Europe:

This winter Dinard will miss one of its best known figures.

> The Reverend J. M. Vallance who has been chaplain here for
> the past six years has left us to take up his duties at Holy
> Trinity, Paddington ... Careless of popularity and of a retir-
> ing nature he nevertheless attracted by his strong personality
> and kindly ways those who had the privilege of coming into
> contact with him, both French and English. A brilliant scho-
> lar, broad-minded, world travelled, he contributed in no small
> measure to knit together a diversity of interests.

Retiring as he was, he seems to have involved himself in
most activities and missed little of the goings-on amongst
the British/American community while exercising a re-
straining influence on the wilder spirits of a carefree Dinard.

Something went wrong with over the appointment of his
replacement, Frank Pickford who, although he agreed to
carry on as before and not to introduce any practices against
the congregation's wishes, finally turned the chaplaincy
down. The Church Committee had even agreed to his request that he should be known as 'rector'. A locum had to
be found for the summer season of 1930 until the Reverend
G. C. Morrow, MA was duly appointed and given permission
to officiate in October 1930. He was the last permanent
chaplain to stay any length of time before being replaced
by the Reverend Walter Green in May 1934.

A change of chaplain did not, however, deter the annual
conference of the jurisdiction of North and Central Europe
from being help in Dinard, at the Gallic Hotel (now an
apartment block) opposite the Casino in June 1930. The
local organiser was General Sir Horace Smith-Dorien who,
with Sir George Curtis seems to have emerged as one of
the most energetic members of St Bartholomew's committee. It proved to be a popular conference with great attention
being paid to personal comforts. 'The accommodation is
really A1, every room has its bathroom,' was one guest's
comment, and, as each chaplaincy committee had contributed towards the cost of the conference, 'only wine,
cigars etc. had to be paid for by those attending'.

In addition to the usual devotional retreat and addresses and a telegram of good wishes from King George V, it is interesting to note the subjects of the addresses. Although we have seen that by this time the Anglican churches in Brittany were on a steep decline, there was a proposal for a separate diocese for North and Central Europe made by the Rural Dean of France, the Reverend Sydney Smith, seconded by the Reverend F. A. Cardew. It was understood that Anglicans in Europe could no longer be managed from a London centred organisation but it would take some time before this proposal would be generally accepted. An ominous lecture, entitled 'Christianity and Patriotism' foresaw the challenges that the new brand of German nationalism would place upon the peoples of Europe and there was a discussion of the opportunities offered to the Mothers' Union in communities where families were separated from each other for much of the year. In the summing up the bishop emphasised that spiritual help offered to visitors from Great Britain, the Dominions and

A peaceful corner of England in Dinard. The English cemetery, complete with lych gate, dedicated in 1931.

St Bartholomew's garden, a popular attraction for tourists and
residents, leading to the British Library.

America and the fact 'that the Church of England is held
in great respect by foreigners.'

The diocesan Church Magazine for Europe contained
many far-sighted articles and comments showing that Anglicans in Europe were not blind to the situation around
them. As early as 1935, an article from Germany warned
that the nation was 'in deadly danger of putting the myth
of race and blood in place of God' and that the Protestant
Churches were denouncing the German State. Clergy were
already being imprisoned and great support was shown for
Jews who were being systematically persecuted. In September 1935 an writer offered hope for their survival as 'the
Jew has made a marvellous fight in the world in all the
ages; and has done it with his hands tied behind him.'

Back in Dinard, a report of the Bishop's Visitation shows
that life was continuing much as usual.

From Paris I went to Dinard where I was the guest of Sir
George and Lady Fowke. [Elsewhere he seems to have stayed

with Royal families!] In addition to the usual Sunday services we had a very well arranged Confirmation.

I greatly admired the English cemetery which has been established at Dinard. A portion of the town cemetery has been allotted to the English-speaking community who have beautified it at considerable cost and have made it look like an English cemetery at home.

The hospitality at Dinard is overwhelming … I am much impressed by the excellent work which Mr & Mrs Morrow are doing in Dinard. On all sides I have heard the keenest appreciation of their presence and influence.

I had an unusual experience at Dinard as Sir George Fowke was able to lend me some suitable clothing and clubs and I played in a match on what I believe to be the prettiest course in Northern France.

I thoroughly enjoyed my visit to Dinard; kindness met me on every side and there was a most excellent feeling of unity in our church work.

Rt. Revd. Staunton Beatty DD
Bishop of Fulham

In 1934, mindful of its informal title of 'British/American Church', the American bishop was invited to Dinard but was unable to come whereupon the Bishop of Fulham stood in for him. The joint relationship seems to have caused no problem at this time and there was no question of the recognition of St Bartholomew's as a fully regular Anglican church although SPG were still unwilling to include it in its annual bulletin of services in Europe.

The Graveyard

For most British/American residents during these years the chief development was the separate English cemetery. In 1929, Mrs Monteith wrote to the Committee suggesting that a fund for the upkeep and maintenance of British/ American graves should be established. The War Graves

The military section of the 'English' cemetery, which includes seamen from HMS *Charybdis* and British, Canadian and New Zealand aircrew.

Commission had been doing their immaculate best to maintain the graves for which they were responsible but this had tended to highlight the poor maintenance of the civilian graves.

The Committee called the 'Graves and Charitable Fund' was then established under the chairmanship of General Sir Horace Smith-Dorien and consisting of General Sir George Fowke, Mr L. Liddell, Colonel the Hon. N. Gatthomer-Hardy, Lt. Col. H. B. Foote and Mr C. P. Hannay. As well as paying for the upkeep of the graveyard, it was hoped that the fund would also offer relief to 'necessitous cases among the Anglo Americans' although this proposal by Sir George Curtis, who in his role as British Vice-Consul, would know of such needs, was not universally approved.

Sir George Curtis, though not a member of the specific committee was the moving force behind the establishment of the English cemetery. He had suggested to the Maire of Dinard as early as 1927 when the graveyard was being extended, that some part might be assigned to the English speaking community. He even went so far as to consult the India Office about the cost of graves in India although it was pointed out to him that labour in India was considerably cheaper.

The Maire agreed to this assignment and then the Reverend G. C. Morrow began an appeal for funds to 'lay out the piece of ground like an English cemetery by creating a separating wall, grass and gravel paths and planting trees and shrubs.' The cemetery was to be non-denominational and the total cost was 30,000 Francs.

It was left to Sir George to propose the finer details of the arrangement and he suggested that the Municipality would be justified in charging an extra sum for those [many] British/Americans not resident in Dinard, 'otherwise the area would soon be filled'. He also wished to alter the French regulations so that the graves should be granted in perpetuity and not for the more usual thirty years. In addition he suggested a surcharge of 10 per cent on the Municipal fee which would form an upkeep fund so that the cemetery would become 'rather a showpiece'.

The cemetery was not the only concern of Sir George. He was also aware of the difficulties of being reliant upon the Municipal hearse. The current one was horse driven and sometimes the horses found it difficult to descend the hill from the church gate without slipping and falling. His suggestion was that St Bartholomew's should buy its own hearse with the spare cash it held so that they could be free to fix their own time for funerals and even use it as a money-making scheme:

The cost of a new hearse is only about 25,000 Francs but I do not think it will be necessary to buy a new engine as, ordinarily the distance to be traversed will be short and the speed slow. It should be possible to buy a good second-hand engine, fix up the chassis with a tray and a canopy and provide a driver's seat for 15,000 Francs. With eight funerals a year and a charge of 500 Francs the money would soon be repaid. Presumably the hearse would be available for hire by French people or by British and American subjects elsewhere. This would be a legitimate church investment.

The cemetery is still with us to-day but alas, the idea of the hearse was rejected. But little did anyone foresee how great would be the need for the cemetery within a dozen years. During the war the victims of the sinking of HMS *Charybdis* were buried in the cemetery along with members of the RAF and now, in this serene and peaceful place there lie almost as many British and Commonwealth servicemen as civilians.

Finance and Pew Rents

The major means of generating income during the period up to the Second World War was still the pew rent. We have already seen that, in Dinard, payment of membership dues qualified worshippers to be voting members of the Association. This was quite contrary to Anglican practice as was the requirement that potential candidates for the chaplaincy should preach a sermon before the congregation on one Sunday before they could be appointed. This common nonconformist practice was beginning to be perceived as giving too much power to seat holders and those who could afford the pew rents and membership fees.

Pew rents were a source of contention in churches everywhere and particularly so in Dinard where many of the visitors were seasonal. This gave rise to a number of complicated rules to meet the varying needs of permanent and temporary residents. For instance, one long meeting in 1932 considered the matter of whether the pews could be sublet in the holder's absence and, if so, did that mean the tenant was deprived of his or her vote at the annual meeting? Over the years many changes in pew rents had been proposed and adopted but, just at the time when they were in fact beginning to be irrelevant, a flat rate for rents irrespective of the holder's status within the community was finally agreed and charged as follows:

	1 year	6 mths	3 mths	2 mths	1 mth
1 seat	Fr 180	Fr 150	Fr 90	Fr 60	Fr 45
2 seats	Fr 270	Fr 190	Fr 135	Fr 90	Fr 65
3 seats	Fr 320	Fr 220	Fr 160	Fr 105	Fr 80
4 seats	Fr 370	Fr 260	Fr 180	Fr 125	Fr 90

It was no doubt a worthy academic exercise but the fall in the numbers of both residents and visitors meant that it was never fully applied. By the mid-1930s the Committee was asking the bishop if he could find a man of private means who would be willing to be chaplain.

The End of an Era

English speaking citizens were beginning to leave Dinard as they read the coming signs, and the remainder of the nineteen-thirties was spent in simply keeping the church going. Church finances were still reasonable however, and it was possible to purchase a new stove and boiler for the church in 1932, which would have to last for many years to come; and to guarantee a stipend to a new chaplain in 1934 of 16,000 Francs. Mr Morrow was offered and accepted the living of Holy Trinity, Paddington, thus following Mr Vallance; and the new chaplain, the Reverend Walter Green, came from the Embassy Church in Paris. He did not stay long however and although he was offered a 'bonus' of 2000 Francs on 26th May 1935 he resigned shortly afterwards.

The departure of the British caused the inevitable reduction of income and on 24th October 1934 Colonel Anson, who had joined the Committee invited the ladies of the church 'to arrange some form of entertainment for the benefit of church funds' but the response was that 'this was impractical at present'. Several changes in membership of the committee came about at this time and a special effort was made to appoint American members of whom Major Marcellan and Mr Howard were two. Although their stay was short-lived, the appointment of Americans was to be important for the continuation of worship in St Bartholomew's during the early years of the war when the United States was a neutral country and their citizens in France were unmolested.

Signs of crisis in church affairs became visible by 1936 when, after the departure of the Reverend Walter Green, St Bartholomew's had to apply to the Comité de Propagande for a grant of aid. The Syndicate voted unanimously 'un guarantie financiere souvent aller jusqu'à cinq mille francs annuellement' until there were more British people in Dinard to support the church. Here is evidence indeed of the good and popular standing of the British community in Dinard. I wonder if any County or Town Council in Britain has ever awarded a similar grant?

This grant only lasted until 1937 and it was only due to the munificence of a new Committee member, Count de Gasquet James, that the Reverend F. Gwynne Davies, the successor to the Reverend Walter Green was given accommodation in the Hotel des Dunes and paid. Gwynne Davies resigned on 30th January 1938 and the Reverend G. H. Johnston became responsible for the services at a salary of Fr 24,000 per annum, plus the Easter collection 'and the chaplain's house as it stands'. This may have been the one loaned to the church by Reggie Forbes. Count de Gasquet James was an American of French descent and with other fellow countrymen was to give support to St Bartholomew's when the British had left. In doing so, he gathered together a number of other Americans living in that part of France, one of whom was to feature significantly in the story of the church during the next decade. In the meantime the church continued although Mr Johnston resigned the chaplaincy exactly one year after his appointment on 31st January 1939.

He was followed by a series of visiting chaplains, including the Reverend N. J. Salmon who, although he had reached the age of 75, applied for the permanent post. At the meeting 'the great majority of the seatholders saw no objection to the age of 75' and it was then decided to ask Mr Morrow to interview Mr Salmon and give his opinion as to whether he thought the applicant would suit Dinard. Mr Morrow presented a positive report and the chaplaincy was offered to Mr Salmon who accepted it.

Unfortunately by March 1939 'friction arose between Mr Salmon and some members of the congregation which led Mr Salmon to offer his resignation.' This was accepted by the Committee who then agreed to pay all expenses incurred by the chaplain in coming over to Dinard. Other members resigned from the committee as a result including a Frenchman, M. Pignatel, leaving only Messrs Hanbury and Hannay as committee members who remained in Dinard. Happily Father Geoffrey Curtis, son of Sir George and Lady Curtis, was available for Holy Week and Easter when 114 communicants were recorded. Though a long way short of the 280 communicants when Father Curtis took the services in 1926, it does show that Dinard was still a favourite centre for English-speaking tourists even so soon before the outbreak of war.

In July 1939 the chaplaincy was accepted by the Reverend C. H. W. Grimes and he was officiating when war was declared on Sunday, 2nd September. There were 300 people at the annual Armistice Day service in November that year indicating the amount of confidence many still had during the period of the 'phony war', and there was even a new chaplain appointed in January 1940 when Mr Grimes left Dinard. The Reverend Hugh David Jones continued to take the services until he too left just before Dunkirk after taking a service of 26th May. On Easter Day that year there were 72 communicants.

Rather charmingly the last minute in St Bartholomew's committee Minute Book after some re-elections was a vote of thanks proposed by the Hon. Treasurer to 'the ladies who so kindly provided and arranged the flowers'. Then the war finally took over.

CHAPTER NINE

The War and
Its Aftermath

France was in a curious position following the defeat of their army and the British evacuation at Dunkirk, by which time all the able-bodied British had left Dinard. Intense propaganda by the victorious Germans had created a strong anti-British sentiment, largely because Great Britain was accused of prolonging the war. In particular, the Americans who were not to join the conflict for another two years were being wooed by the Germans in an attempt to keep them out of the war altogether. As a result, even while the Battle of Britain was being fought over the skies of Kent and London, regular Anglican services were being maintained at St Bartholomew's by a newcomer who arrived in Dinard at a propitious moment, Colonel Karl Cate.

Colonel Cate was an American who worked in Paris but owned a chateau a few miles outside Dinard. He discovered the existence of St Bartholomew's and immediately became involved just before the war. He had been an ordained priest of the Episcopal Church but gave up his Orders at the end of the First World War owing to some intellectual difficulties. However at this time of crisis on the departure of the English chaplains, he took over the running of the church for a few months and the last entry in the church register on 27th October 1940 records that there were 23 people attending Matins. He may have continued to conduct services beyond this date which have not been recorded.

One of the remaining British residents was Johnny Clark

who stayed on to look after the church during the Occupation and it must be largely due to him that St Bartholomew's
remained in such good order during the war.

On the arrival of the occupying forces, it was agreed that
an English service might be held at 10 a.m. which would
be followed by a Lutheran service for German servicemen
at 11.00 a.m. The arrangement seems to have worked well
with mutual respect shown by the respective congregations.
The story is told that, during the final hymn at the English
service the verger, Johnny Clark, would throw open the
porch doors outside which the young German soldiers were
waiting. As the hymn was being sung the Germans would
spring to attention. After some weeks of this the chosen
hymn became No. 707 in Hymns Ancient and Modern,
'God save our gracious King'. As the congregation left the
soldiers would remain at attention before going into church
for their service. If the story is accurate, it is a small but
significant example of Christian courtesy being displayed
even in times of war and mutual malevolence.

A similar incident took place a few miles over the channel
in occupied Guernsey when the rector of St Peter in the
Wood, Canon Spencer Gerhold, chose the National Anthem
during an evening of hymn singing led by a young German
organist. He was immediately deported to a concentration
camp as a punishment.

Not all was peaceful co-operation however, and Elizabeth
Hannay provided an example of the determined resilience
of the people left behind. Mrs Adelaide Spofford, a long-
term resident who was not going to leave her home for
anyone, was giving a dinner party during the early days of
the occupation when there was a knock on her front door.
She went to answer it and found a German officer on the
doorstep.

'I want you to give permission to billet German soldiers
in your house,' he said.

'I live in a conquered country,' replied Mrs Spofford, 'You are our conquerors. You may do as you wish and billet German soldiers in my house but it will not be with my permission.' No Germans were ever billeted on her and she remained in Dinard throughout the war, becoming a member of the reconstituted Church Committee at the Liberation.

Members of Dinard church also played their heroic part in the Resistance, which became so strong and militant in Brittany. Many memorials outside parish churches testify to the numbers shot by the Germans for their brave resistance in the Occupation. One member of St Bartholomew's to join the Resistance was Virginie d'Albert who spent her war years leading escaping RAF aircrew and other prisoners of war to safety from one collection point to another on her bicycle. She was finally captured by the Gestapo and sentenced to Ravensbruck Concentration Camp where she suffered illness and depredation but eventually returned to her equally brave husband. There is a memorial hassock to her in the church and it is hoped that there will be a more permanent memorial to her in due course.

As a precaution Johnny Clark hid the communion vessels in his garden during the Occupation but it is notable that, when the war ended it was found that the Germans had left everything in immaculate order. All the registers and records were found to be intact and not a book or ornament was missing. In fact the only damage to the church happened during the bombing of St Malo docks by the RAF when a stray bomb landed in Dinard and the north-east window next to the organ was blown out. Fortunately this was one of the only plain glass windows in the church, so little was lost. It is now filled with the St Bartholomew window, designed, made and donated by the Pierpont family and dedicated by Bishop Frank Sargeant on St Bartholomew's Day, 2001.

Services recorded in the registers resumed on 25th August 1946 when Colonel Cate once more officiated and 24 attended Matins. The entry in the register continues where it left off on 27th October 1940 without any comment about what had happened in the meantime. Likewise the Committee Minute Book takes up where it left off on 3rd December 1939 when it states that on 24th September 1946 members of the Committee were able to meet for the first time 'since the war had interrupted the church services' and there were present Count de Gasquet James, Mrs Forbes and Mr Kendrick.

It was also recorded that 'the church has been spared all but minor damage during the war and appreciation of the tenacious attitude of J. Clark during the occupation and of his care of the church were expressed … Certain funds of the church were being used for relief work … and a present of 1500 Francs was given to Pasteur Poulin who had conducted church services during his holiday in Dinard' (presumably during the summer of 1946).

It is perhaps appropriate at this distance to express the gratitude of church members to the German padres and soldiers who used St Bartholomew's for prayer and worship for their care and respect for the fabric and ornaments of the church.

At the first post-war meeting the Committee agreed that 'the church is likely to remain inactive during the winter months.' A totally new era in the life of St Bartholomew's was about to begin.

Post-war renewal

Just as the church registers record a continuity with the past without reference to the war, so the Committee quickly re-established itself and began to plan for the future. Mr W. A. Kendrick, who had been a member since 1926 felt unable to carry on and Mr C. P. Hannay also resigned on 4th September 1948. They were replaced by Lady Curtis and Mrs Adelaide Spoffard who had resided in Dinard throughout the war.

Happily the church finances were found to be intact and it was found that the 7000 Francs remaining in the deposit account from 1939 had now grown to 92,000 Francs. The total assets of the church now amounted to 130,000 Francs of which 36,000 belonged to the cemetery fund. Moreover all expenses incurred during and after the occupation had been fully paid. Alas this dramatic rise in the paper value of the assets had more to do with the collapse in the value of the franc than with any real increase in value but at least

Elizabeth Hannay in her 'atelier', the place of many meetings with people from all over the world. The bust in the upper background is that of Sir George Curtis.

the finances were in the 'black'. The church was able to plan more positively for the future than the other remaining Anglican churches on account of its local management and independence.

The severely reduced Anglo-American population in Dinard meant that the Committee had to agree that the church should open only during the summer months from June to October 'in the interim' and chaplains should be invited for 'holiday duty', paid for by the Association, and put up in local hotels. Invitations were to be extended from time to time to Anglo-Catholic priests but, in general, the services should continue to reflect the Broad Church tradition with Morning Prayer and Holy Communion held at the 10.45 a.m. hour on Sundays. No doubt the Committee were bearing in mind the readiness of Father Geoffrey Curtis of the Mirfield fathers to help out from time to time, which persuaded them to modify the rules about churchmanship.

Choice of chaplains seem to have been a haphazard affair in these immediate post-war days and one, the Reverend W. Davies was appointed having 'met Lady Curtis by chance' in the street. But by 1950 the Bishop of Fulham was actively involved in finding chaplains and the Committee even approached the Colonial and Continental Church Society, although they do not appear to have offered any chaplains. Whether this was on account of the primarily evangelical persuasion of their members or for some other reason is not known. Visiting clergy were put up in the Grand Hotel, the Falaise or the Roche Corneille, the latter being the preferred place on account of its convenience and cheapness. Later on a deal was done by which the chaplain was offered free accommodation there in return for the free use of the church garden by the residents of the hotel. This arrangement lasted until the early 1970s although two of the chaplains, including Donald Pankhurst recall that the chaplain's rooms were in the servants' quarters.

By 1950 Miss Elizabeth Hannay, who was now playing a leading part in the running of St Bartholomew's, was able to announce that the organ had been completely overhauled and was now in good condition. There was even a discussion about the possibility of a chaplain's residence being built on the site originally bought for the purpose half a century before, between the church and the rue Clemenceau (where the present block of apartments containing the chaplain's flat now stands).

At this time the majority of the Committee held American citizenship including Count de Gasquay James (although of French descent), Elizabeth Hannay and Adelaide Spofford, in addition to Colonel Cate who had been elected president. Mr Reginald Forbes (Reggie) received his income from the United States and this renewed the uncertainty about where St Bartholomew's stood in relation to the Church of England and its sister American Episcopal Church in Europe. Also there was an occasional misunderstanding arising from its adopted description of 'The British-American Church' of Dinard, which led to its being considered a non-denominational church for the benefit of English speaking people.

Matters came to a head when, in 1949, Colonel Cate wrote to the Bishop of Fulham suggesting that the Reverend J. W. Dunbar should be appointed as chaplain to Dinard during the summer months and to Biarritz during the winter. This presumption by a lay member of the committee at Dinard to try and arrange matters for other parts of the diocese in Europe, sensible as it may have been, was too much for Bishop Selwyn. 'What they did at Dinard is their own affair', grumbled the Bishop 'but in any event, [he] would not approve of Dunbar going to Biarritz '.

A confidential report by Bishop Selwyn of a meeting with Colonel Cate at Bishop Chambers' flat in Paris on Monday, 3rd April 1950 reveals something of the situation and status of St Bartholomew's during these years.

Colonel Cate had emphatically pointed out that Mr Dunbar's ministry in Dinard the previous year had been very successful. It had been arranged that he should have free accommodation in various hotels so that 'he could get to know visitors' and, as a result 'the church was very well attended and he was entirely acceptable'. He held an early morning communion service and at 10.45 a.m. he conducted Morning Prayer followed by Holy Communion according to the wishes of the committee.

> The congregation is composed of all denominations but Colonal Cate said that the form of service was according to the Book of Common Prayer [wrote Bishop Selwyn]. When I asked him if there was intercommunion [at this time banned in the Church of England] he could not say for certain but he assumed that this was not so as only six to eight people stayed on for the Celebration after Morning Service.
>
> When Colonel Cate asked me what objection there was to Dunbar I said I could hardly discuss this but that he held no licence from the Bishop of London to officiate on the Continent, that there might be reasons why we should prefer him not to and that the position was somewhat awkward seeing that he had been taken on to the staff of the American Cathedral in Paris without any arrangements being made by us ...
>
> ... My impressions of Colonel Cate are that he is a perfectly sincere and conscientious man who is genuinely desirous of securing proper administration at Dinard. He may, of course, not fully understand the Anglican position but he seemed perfectly reasonable and willing to acquiesce in any steps which the Bishop of London would wish to take to regularise the whole situation.

His report goes on to say that 'the church is governed by a committee elected from the church community which consists of those who contribute 100 Francs per year. This of course is now absurd as after devaluation this is the equivalent of 2/– (i.e. 10 pence).

The Bishop of London's desire to 'regularise' the situation was underlined by the Bishop of Fulham who wrote to the Committee objecting to the appointment of the Reverend Dunbar in spite of failing to obtain the Bishop of London's approval. While acknowledging the right of the Committee to appoint their own chaplains, he emphasised once again the requirement to obtain the approval of the Bishop of London, 'no matter who is the patron. This is in line with the practice of the Anglican Communion all the world over, in America, I imagine as well as in England, namely that every appointment must have the sanction of the Bishop.'

He continued by conceding that the Committee was perfectly in order in selecting Mr Dunbar and that there was probably a misunderstanding because, 'in the previous year the then Bishop of Fulham said that his approval was unnecessary or words to that effect.' It was an unfortunate mistake because all Anglican chaplaincies in North and Central Europe are in the jurisdiction of the Bishop of London.

The Bishop then explained to the Committee that the Bishop of London, together with the Bishop of Fulham and Bishop Chambers had come to the conclusion that they could not give permission to the Reverend Dunbar to officiate. The decision 'was not taken lightly' although they did not wish to go into details. He further explained that Bishops have access to information which members of a committee cannot have and that such a step was taken simply and solely in the interest of the Church as a whole and the work of the church on the Continent. 'If they will consider this, I believe that they will, though sorely disappointed, loyally accept the position.'

Elsewhere the same bishop wrote about the list of banned chaplains and that 'there are sundry parsons who are unsatisfactory and are always trying for jobs on the Continent.

I know many of them and if you are to ask me, I can probably tell you about them as they crop up.' In addition he warned that the Colonial and Continental Church Society have to be watched 'as they tend to send out their own supporters who are often aged gentlemen and not all of them are very good, though they are taking more care.'

Later the same bishop left a confidential memorandum for his successor which throws further light on St Bartholomew's at this time:

> Dinard is in a somewhat curious position. Administered by an Anglo-American committee which, according to its statutes have the right to appoint seasonal chaplains, generally Easter and then June to mid-September.
>
> A few years ago a difficult situation arose owing to my refusal to accept an impossible man, but that is now all over and relations are very happy.
>
> The key man is Mr Karl Cate, an American ... He works very hard at the arrangements and is a good and sincere man but is inclined to interpret the position of the Church at Dinard rather too widely and would himself favour what amounts to interdenominationalism. But I think he has got this straight now and in practice there should be no difficulty. Nevertheless it must be borne in mind that there is at least one French Protestant on the committee.
>
> I have tried to persuade Cate that his best plan is to let me know the men he would like to invite so that I may check them up and advise him as to which are the best before he writes to them and this I have done to some extent for the coming summer. He has by now a pretty good list which includes some who have been several times.
>
> In Dinard you will find yourself in another world, that is as far as the residents go. Lady Curtis sometimes gets worried about Cate's handling of affairs because she is a good churchwoman and has a son who is a Mirfield Father. Lady Burton, an American widow, is a great character. The best of the whole bunch is Elizabeth Hannay who is a great peacemaker, tremendously efficient and can be trusted absolutely.

If ever there are any difficulties I should never hesitate to consult her. Her mother is an American widow.

The sexton, Johnny Clark, is a great character ... He can be awkward if he takes a dislike to someone but Elizabeth Hannay can always handle him.

It was a vigorously active time for St Bartholomew's although the resident English/American congregation was small, and it is a great tribute to the management that while all the other Anglican churches in the area were either closing or totally dependent on SPG support in order to remain open at all, the church not only remained entirely self-supporting but also attracted growing numbers of visitors during the summer months. Mr Brooks, who was travelling administrator in Europe for both SPG and the Colonial and Continental Church Society sent a report in the autumn of 1952 to the effect that:

Although the number of visitors is smaller owing to the reduced holiday allowances, yet the congregations at St Bartholomew's have been excellent and the collections considerably in excess of last year's. A new window has been placed in the transept in memory of a devoted member of the congregation, Florence de Bray, who was English by birth and married to a Frenchman. The window is somewhat modern in design and depicts Our Lord welcoming the children. This is particularly appropriate in a resort where hundreds of children bathe and play all the day long. A sacred concert was held in August and raised £17 towards the upkeep of graves in the civilian British cemetery, where in many cases all traces of relations have been lost and the graves have sadly deteriorated. And this, it has to be said, was achieved in spite of the failure of the Jurisdiction and SPG to advertise the church services at Dinard in the annual holiday advertisement which was intended to cover all Anglican chaplaincies in Europe.

The close contact with the Bishop of Fulham, the changing

membership of the Committee, the new situation in post-war France and the desire of church members to be part of the overlapping jurisdiction of the Episcopal Church of the United States meant that the time had come to have another look at the Constitution of St Bartholomew's to make it more secure for the years to come.

The Statutes Revised

The first and most controversial amendment proposed by the Committee was aimed at 'wielding together the elements which now compose the church congregation' by altering Article One. This had stated that the Bishop of London alone had authority to licence or give permission for a chaplain to officiate 'according to the tenets of the Established Church of England'. Now the Committee wanted to extend this authority to the Bishop in charge of Protestant Episcopal Churches (of the USA) in Europe.

A useful and helpful response was received from the Bishop of Fulham who clarified the situation, although it has to be said, it left the church in Dinard in an ambiguous situation which has only now been satisfactorily resolved.

After a reference to past relations with the Bishop of London and the close co-operation with the jurisdiction of North and Central Europe, the bishop goes on:

> The suggestion that the constitution should be altered so that the American Episcopal Bishop in Europe should share the appointment with the Bishop of London (not the Bishop of Fulham who only acts for London) seems to be both unnecessary and beyond the powers of the members of the church.
>
> **Unnecessary** because, if the wording of the clause is as I have quoted it, the appointment is in the hands of the Committee and not of the Bishop. The Bishop has to approve.
>
> **Beyond the powers of the church members**, because

Dinard is in the jurisdiction of the Bishop of London and he could not, even if he wished to, give up any share or part of his jurisdiction. The American Episcopal Church is in the Anglican Communion. It has its own particular spheres of jurisdiction. So too the Episcopal churches of the Dominions. I imagine the only exceptions are the American churches e.g. at Paris. If a church is called an 'Anglo-American Church' I still do not think there could be any dual Episcopal control. Dinard has always recognised the jurisdiction of the Bishop of London and I do not think any alteration of the constitution would be valid.

The bishop went on to reassure the American members recalling the fact that 'one man selected by the Committee was unsuitable' does not invalidate the rights of the Committee. It is a most unusual occurrence and therefore never likely to happen again.'

The clause was dropped from the statutes but the point was made to the effect that St. Bartholomew's has been enriched by the regular participation of chaplains from the United States and visits from the American bishop in Europe as well as bishops and clergy from Provinces outside the Church of England, such as New Zealand, Australia, Wales, Scotland and Ireland. Permission to officiate has always been given.

The other alterations to the constitution were more important in that they concerned the status of the church in French law. The most significant of these was to pass a resolution filing an application with the sous-Prefect of St Malo as an 'association cultuelle' rather than an 'association ordinaire'. The difference is that an 'association cultuelle' can receive alms, gifts and legacies without tax penalties and without special authorisation. The only drawback was that reserve funds had to be limited to three times the annual average expenditure and excess reserves had to be deposited with the 'Caisse des depots et consignations' to be used exclusively for repairs, constructions and purchase of equipment. In fact this suited the needs of St Bartholomew's admirably.

The end of the post-war era

Although official relations with the diocese seem to have been severed, the close, informal relationships with the Bishop remained as warm as ever. When the Bishop of Fulham visited Dinard in 1953 and enjoyed the traditional hospitality offered to visiting bishops, this time at the hands of Lady Burton and Colonel and Mrs Karl Cate, he wrote of the support given to the church 'by the no means numerous Anglo-American community' and the strength of the summer congregations. He recorded the testimonial gift given to Johnny Clark and the certificate (now hanging in the church vestry) which records his devoted service to the church. Of significance too is the mention of the re-dedication of Paramé Church after the compensation for war damage had repaired it but correctly cast doubts on its ability to survive. He also felt that 'buses can bring people into Dinard where there is every prospect of St Bartholomew's continuing to flourish every summer. Certainly it deserves to'. At last here is an indication of official recognition of the strength and importance of St Bartholomew's as a 'loved church' and the likelihood of its being the last remaining Anglican church in Brittany.

Shortly afterwards Colonel Cate resigned from the Committee having seen the church through the worst years of the war and having helped to ensure its survival. He returned to Paris and soon we find him on the Council of the Anglican church at Maison Lafitte near Versailles, which is described as 'being more Protestant than Catholic' and therefore more to his liking.

For years to come St Bartholomew's continued through the summer season, opening at Easter with a grand spring clean and then continuing through the summer from Whit-sun to the end of September with visiting chaplains. But a new inspiration emerged to enlarge its mission and contact with the wider church, led and meticulously managed by one person above all, Miss Elizabeth Hannay.

This was partly inspired by a remarkable example of goodwill and practical help from the local Roman Catholic parish when, years before the general opening of ecumenical activity, the Curé of Dinard, L'Abbé Peletier ministered to the needs of the remaining members of the British/American colony. In particular Mass was held on the day of the funerals of King George VI in 1952 and of old Queen Mary in 1953 and he allowed the regular worshippers at St Bartholomew's to receive the Holy Communion in the Roman Catholic church when there was no Anglican priest available. Without doubt St Bartholomew's belonged to the whole Christian community in Dinard and the Anglican church became the centre of the ecumenical movement which attracted all the main Christian groups around the banks of the River Rance.

CHAPTER TEN

Vision and Growing Strength

Ecumenism

In the years after the war and before the Second Vatican Council there was a growing awareness of the need for Christians to rediscover their common faith and unite in debating the issues which threatened to marginalise their beliefs in an age which was already pointing towards a post-Christian Western world. Before the 1950s the Churches took pains to emphasise their differences and to assert their own theological positions over against their neighbours while giving little more than lip-service to the challenge of Church Unity. Many religious attitudes at the time throughout the Christian world were not so very different from those we deplore in Northern Ireland up to the present time.

In France the situation was such that it must have seemed unlikely that a movement for Church Unity would find any impetus. The Roman Catholic Church was universal and all-embracing in every region except Alsace where Protestants were the majority. Few French people had ever come across the Anglican or Orthodox Churches and the question of Church Unity was hardly a matter for urgent consideration amongst the other pressing religious concerns. Yet it was in France that the modern ecumenical movement can be said to have started, thanks to the vision of a very special

priest, Paul Couturier. It was he who founded the Week of
Prayer for Christian Unity ending with the Feast of St Paul
on January 25th and encouraged his fellow Christians to
pray not for the unity they thought best for the Church but
for 'unity as and how Christ wills.'

In Dinard we have already seen how the Abbé Le Peletier,
Curé of Notre Dame, had accepted responsibility for the
moral and spiritual care of Anglicans who were deprived of
their chaplain after the war, by a spontaneous act of gesture
of Christian friendship. As a result he met Father Geoffrey
Curtis during his visits to take charge of St Bartholomew's
and to see his mother, Lady Curtis. The two spent long
hours together discussing the nature of the Church and
how they might help to bring about a greater understanding
between Anglicans and Catholics. They decided that they
must invite the faithful of the two denominations to unite
together in prayer to hasten the 'hour of unity'. The first
meeting was arranged for 23rd March 1958. Father Le Peletier died before the dream was realised but the meeting was
held, the seed was sown and it was soon to appear.

In the meantime, Elizabeth Hannay had read the bio-
graphy of L'Abbé Couturier by Père Villain and together
with the new Curé of Notre Dame, she went and rang the
local Protestant pastor's doorbell. Thus was born the 'groupe
oecumenique des bords de la Rance' which quickly gathered
some forty members at its monthly meetings consisting of
Anglicans, Catholics, Protestants and Orthodox. From the
start they not only prayed together but aimed to 'confront
real problems' and to co-operate wherever possible. The
Week of Prayer for Christian Unity, as elsewhere, became
a special occasion for active participation in each other's
services and at Christmas a combined poster was produced
reminding all Christians of the spiritual nature of the
Nativity.

Leading members of the Ecumenical Movement were

invited as speakers and in those early years such well-known names as Père Villain, friend and biographer of Paul Couturier, Father Kniazeff, Orthodox leader in Paris, and the Biblical scholar, Pasteur Baral appeared in Dinard. The Groupe Oecumenique also received messages of encouragement from Michael Ramsay, Archbishop of Canterbury and Pope John XXIII.

But this was not sufficient for the leading motivator, Miss Hannay, who in addition to helping keep St Bartholomew's alive, saw that the Anglicans were also in a position to further the cause of unity. In 1960 St Andrew's church, Saint Lunaire was up for sale by SPG and she seized her opportunity. 'She rang the alarm bells. "Are we going to allow the church to become a gymnasium or a dance hall?" she asked.' She rattled the nerves of the Anglican authorities and won a reprieve for the church.

The church was in a bad state but the Groupe recruited a team of young Catholic and Protestant volunteers, mostly from S. Servan to restore and refurbish the church. The result was remarkable and the church was divided into two parts, one with a simple altar for prayer and offices, the other for meetings. On its completion in 1962 the Anglican chaplain of St Bartholomew's rededicated the church, the Mother Superior of an Anglican convent rang the Angelus of Resurrection on the newly installed bell and all the congregation of whom the greater part were Catholics, joined together in the office. Soon after regular Eucharists were held for Anglican and Orthodox holiday-makers. At the time it was a remarkable venture and attracted much attention from the French press.

With characteristic energy Elizabeth also encouraged members of the Groupe to gain wider experience by arranging pilgrimages to other parts of France, first to L'Abbaye du Bec at Lyon, in memory of Paul Couturier and later to Chartres, and the Protestant community at Taizé. The climax came with a much larger pilgrimage, joined by many English Catholics to spiritual centres of France, starting from le Mont St Michel and going on to Solesmes, Mans, Nevers, Paray-le-Moniel, Taize, Lyons and Vezalay in 1966.

Although the centre at St Lunaire no longer exists and the library and other materials was brought to St Bartholomew's to be housed in the ecumenical library there where they have remained until recently, the work continued to prosper and takes its place alongside those other initiatives in many parts of the world which have led to greater understanding, practical co-operation and a common theological language which is now a familiar part of Christian church life.

Elizabeth Hannay's ecumenical work was acknowledged and respected on both sides of the Channel, when she was appointed as one of the Anglican members of the Anglican/Roman Catholic conversations in France and a report by Canon Senior records the activities of the 'vigorous Ecumenical group of which Miss Hannay is the chairman and inspiration. She is a devotee of the late Father Geoffrey Curtis CR and is clearly seen as an Anglican, respected by the RCs and French Reformed and other traditions.'

Ecumenical Visits

Perhaps as a result of this active search for Christian Unity in the Dinard area, though the initial source of the initiative remains unknown, the Reverend Alan Charters, then Chaplain of Elizabeth College, Guernsey, was invited to give talks to French Catholic clergy who wanted to know more about the Anglican Church. His first visit was during the Week of Prayer for Christian Unity in January 1966 when he stayed with the Abbé Maurice Chevalier in St Brieuc and then went on to Guingamp. Dinard was not visited on this occasion as, of course, the church was closed during the

Eric Waddams rehearsing the Elizabeth College Chapel Choir, Guernsey, for a performance of English church music on French television. He was one of four brothers who were choristers, then choral scholars of King's College, Cambridge.

winter months. Later in the same year, the choir of Elizabeth College, where the redoubtable Eric Waddams was Director of Music, visited the area with the chaplain, singing liturgical services in Roman Catholic churches and cathedrals. Eric was a remarkable musician from a remarkable family. He and his three brothers were all choristers and then choral scholars of King's College, Cambridge under the legendary choirmaster, Boris Ord who set the standard of the cathedral music of his day. During his time Eric sent a steady trickle of organ and choral scholars to Oxford and Cambridge colleges which was a remarkable achievement in a fairly isolated island far away from the centres of cathedral excellence. Such was the interest in this choir venture that French television produced a half hour programme of music by the choir, recorded in Paramé Roman Catholic church.

It was also in 1966 that the choir enjoyed the privilege of joining the choir of Winchester cathedral and the Benedictine monks to sing the first Mass in the Abbey of Mont St Michel to be allowed since the Napoleonic regime and then to sing Anglican Evensong during the afternoon of this celebration of the thousandth anniversary of the foundation.

So successful were these visits that they became regular events and French Catholic congregations clearly appreciated the distinct contribution that the unique Anglican choral tradition made to liturgical worship. One musical curate of Pleurtuit, the Abbé Yves Perrault, who has since become a close friend of the author, founded a parish choir and soon entered the National French Choral Competition

The Archduke and Duchess Vladimir Romanov, head of the Russian royal family outside St Bartholomew's after attending Easter Eucharist in 1986. With him are members of the King's School, Gloucester, of which Alan Charters was headmaster.

The choir of the King's School, Gloucester, led by the charismatic
Director of Music Ian Fox, who have been regular visitors to St
Bartholomew's for Holy Week and Easter.

which was held in the south of France in 1969. One of the
pieces of music chosen for the competition was a carol he
had heard sung by the Elizabeth College choir during a
concert of music for the Church seasons. It was 'Ding dong
merrily on high' and Pleurtuit won the competition! It was
a special delight when, years later Alan Charters was appointed to the Cure of Souls at St Bartholomew's in 2000,
he found Yves Perrault, the curate of Pleurtuit, had become
Dean and Curé of Notre Dame, Dinard.

Unfortunately English educational theory ceased to believe that children could grow in experience and knowledge
outside the classroom, so the idea that young people might
be allowed to vanish from school on a foreign choir tour
during term time became unfashionable. As a result the
choir changed its visits to the holiday period of Holy Week
and Easter, at the same time making St Bartholomew's its
base for the first time in 1971 and staying at the then

monastery St Francois in the Vicomté. This gave the opportunity to visit more churches for the Holy Week services as well as helping the young choristers to understand and involve themselves in this most important week of the Christian year.

As Alan Charters moved on to other schools so the choirs of St John's, Leatherhead and the King's School, the cathedral school of Gloucester visited Dinard in turn. Many people in Brittany remember with affection the enthusiastic and sometimes brilliant directorship of the charismatic Ian Fox who was himself an assistant cathedral organist before moving on to Gloucester. On one occasion the Cathedral choir made a tour, under the expert direction of John Sanders, culminating in the Toussaints Mass at St Malo Cathedral at which the Reverend Alan Charters preached.

Those visits together with the more important work of the Groupe Oecumenique along with similar activities continuing in many parts of the world, have led to the conviction that the most important and immediate aims of the Ecumenical Movement must be to achieve sincere friendship and respect for each other's traditions at a local level, rather than the formal negotiations for reunion which was once the purpose. As it happened the present writer has concelebrated the Mass many times with fellow Roman Catholic priests, on one occasion with Cardinal Gouyon who was responsible for the Roman Catholic contribution to the ecumenical movement in France and more recently with the Archbishop of Bourges, while priests from Dinard have celebrated the Anglican Eucharist in England without any sense of embarrassment or wrong-doing. Church unity will come from below rather than from institutional decrees from above.

It was however not all plain sailing. When Alan Charters was invited to go to Rennes in the late 1960s to visit L'Abbé Bernard Poirier, a theologian at the Grand Seminaire, and to meet Cardinal Gouyon he felt he needed some support. He invited his diocesan bishop of Winchester, the Right Reverend Faulkner Allison to join the group. The two bishops took to each other at once and there is an abiding memory of the cardinal and the bishop walking round the cloisters of the Grand Seminaire arm in arm, each with a little pocket dictionary which they consulted from time to time during their animated conversations. The visit, including Mass at Rennes Cathedral, was considered a great success with the meeting of leading churchmen from France and England. However, when the visit was reported, there was a thunderbolt from the Bishop of Gibraltar in Europe, reminding us that he was the bishop with authority in France and it was quite wrong to invite the Bishop of Winchester to usurp his rightful position.

One significant outcome of these choir visits, apart from the opportunity to share the worship of other churches was that, at the last count, some twenty-seven of Alan Charters' former pupils are now priests and one is a monk. Many of these took part in the choirs which visited St Bartholomew's and the Roman Catholic churches of the area.

The Last Years of the Twentieth Century

Although in these years, use of St Bartholomew's was restricted to a few summer months during the season, the congregations were large and the church retained its loyal, long-serving members while attracting new worshippers. From the moment it became a church there has been a long tradition of committed and expert management by lay people who grew to love the church and the community it gathered and the lean years after the war were no exception. Apart from Elizabeth Hannay, Bill Channing, who became President up to and beyond the Hundredth Anniversary celebrations in 1971, played a significant part in maintaining good relations with the Diocese in Europe as well as ensuring that the church remained in satisfactory repair. François and Betty Paquement were also stalwart supporters at this time, although they lived in Paris for most of the year and they were largely responsible for keeping St Bartholomew's financially solvent. Madame Beau is another well-known and long-standing church member who has looked after the fabric and general well-being of the building.

One of the most valued features of the church is the library which has developed over the years with a wide range of titles for the benefit of English readers and is well used by residents and visitors. In recent years this has been greatly improved by Henry and Eileen Spenceley who took charge of it and reordered and recatalogued the books. In 2002 the whole library was restored and repainted with new shelves and essential damp-proofing. The existing ecumenical library, consisting mostly of volumes in French dating from the early years of the movement has been moved to the public library for security where researchers can work in better conditions.

Quite apart from the essential business of providing the means of regular worship and the provision of chaplains the Committee has continued to be responsible for maintaining the rights and obligations of St Bartholomew's in French law along with due regard to the diocese and the Anglican Communion. Examples of this are the long and protracted case in the 1960s when a court case brought by M. et Mme. Bouvet claimed rights of land and passage on part of land belonging to St Bartholomew's. The persistent and accurate argument based on evidence from Elizabeth Hannay and others, saw off the opponents in such a manner that the litigants were fined in the Appeal Court at Rennes for their 'action vexatoire' which led to St Bartholomew's being awarded 'dommages and interets' to the extent of 650 New Francs (approx £65).

During the post-war years, St Bartholomew's found it necessary to help out the remaining neighbouring Anglican churches to a considerable extent, in particular Dinan, which though closed for many years was still the responsibility of the Anglican church and St Lunaire. Dinan church alone cost St Bartholomew's 424.24 Francs per year in insurance during the six years before its sale. It was Bill Channing who battled hard to extract money which the diocese had received from the sale of Christchurch on account of 'having borne the considerable costs of the maintenance of Dinan' claiming that 'for this reason both the previous bishops, Roger Cooke and Alan Rogers stated that any monies gained from the sale of the property [at Dinan] could be used by St Bartholomew's for so long as it was operating as a church but should revert to the Bishop of Fulham if at any time St Bartholomew's ceased to function as a church.' This together with the war reparations that were also given to Dinan in the 1950s would help to keep an important physical presence for the Church of England in this area of France.

No capital sum was ever received but in 1977 a loan of 20,000 Francs was offered by the Diocese at a rate of 6 per cent per annum for ten years. SPG had also offered a loan at 10 per cent over 5 years. The latter was declined.

At the same time, in response to a request from Bill Channing, Canon Harold Isherwood wrote a letter to the French authorities and the British Inland Revenue on behalf of covenanted donations given to St Bartholomew's:

> This is to certify that the British American Church at Dinard, France is a recognised Anglican Church and is in the Diocese of the Bishop of Fulham and Gibraltar.
>
> Apart from the collections from the faithful, they have no other support. Some members and friends of the church occasionally make small annual contributions. The church can be considered for all purposes as a charitable institution.

It can be seen from the story so far that to be President of the Association of St Bartholomew's was never going to be a sinecure and could be very demanding indeed. But it has always been the case that the church has never lacked able lay leaders and a new family appeared on the scene in the early 1970s to whom St Bartholomew's owes an immense amount. From the moment they arrived Julian and Audrey Thompson threw themselves into the life of the church, at first cleaning, organising the flowers and the doing the multitude of routinely obscure jobs demanded of every parish.

But quite soon, Julian helped to fulfil a dream the Committee had had since the Reverend Percy Clarke was chaplain the late 1890s. The ground at the west end between the church and the rue Georges Clemenceau, originally purchased for the parsonage, was sold to a construction firm S. A. Royale for development which was to include a flat for the chaplain of St Bartholomew's with access to the

Julian Thompson, Sybil Fagg, lay reader, Audrey Thompson, with the American Bishop in Europe, the Right Reverend Jeffrey Rowthorn and the chaplain.

church and leaving a right of passage for pedestrians from the road ro the church. The notice board on the side of the Roche Corneille which had been there since 1924 at the instigation of Colonel Foote was to remain in place. The contract was signed on 2nd February 1981 between the Association de l'Eglise Anglicane represented by François Paquement and Julian Thompson and later, Elizabeth Hannay and François Paquement and signed the flat agreement. At long last there was a permanent home for the chaplain and a further enticement for a clergyman to take his summer holidays with a 'flat for duty' to maintain the services in Dinard.

The Latest Decade

It was soon realised that the apartment was a vital necessity for the future for a new and not entirely expected development took place which meant that a more structured ordering of St Bartholomew's was needed so that the spiritual needs of the British/American community could be catered for. At the end of the 1980s and throughout the 1990s a new migration from mainland Britain to Brittany has taken place ... From 1985 to the time of writing 98 per cent of foreign buyers in the Ille et Villaine departement have been British while the Cotes d'Armor is close behind with 94 per cent British buyers. Of these some 55 per cent have come from the south-east of England with only 4 per cent from Wales and a mere smattering from Scotland. Surprisingly only 6 per cent are retired people with the majority still at work with roughly one third in the 20–40 age group and one third being 40–50. However detailed surveys by the French authorities show that eight out of ten buyers consider their houses in Brittany as second homes and that one third of these intend to sell up and return to Britain within 5–10 years. Even in the fairly settled Franco-

François and Elizabeth Paquement outside the church porch. They helped to keep the church going during the most difficult years.

British world of today there is no long-term certainty of a permanent British migration, although it is quite different from the nineteenth-century migration of the upper classes. The new settlers wish to avoid creating a British ghetto as was nearly the case during La Belle Époque but many find that difficulties of language cut them off from the local life. It is significant that the majority of new British settlers watch British television, relayed on from the Channel Islands and read English newspapers in preference to French ones. They are here because they are seeking a quality of life which is perceived as having died out across the Channel but is still present in Brittany. Above all there is more space and better opportunities to buy old and individual property. Most of the incomers are prepared to take lower status jobs for the opportunity of settling in Brittany. At the time of writing, French census details record some 35,000 British citizens living more or less permanently in Brittany.

St Bartholomew's church has discovered a new purpose as a result of this new colonisation. The small number of

Donald and Heather Pankhurst, whose service to St Bartholomew's
covered thirty years from 1971.

British, American and French families who kept the church
alive for so many years after the Second World War have
been joined by a large number of incomers. And just at the
moment when such a person was most needed, Sybil Fagg,
a licensed Lay Reader has come in to take charge of the
ordering of worship and much other administration. As well
as her liturgical and theological expertise, she was for some
years the Stewardship advisor for the diocese of Southwark
and has rapidly become an indispensable member of the
church. It was Julian and Andrey Thompson with Sybil who
reopened the church for a full range of services throughout
the year for the first time since the Second World War.

Of course St Bartholomew's benefited from the expansion
of British residents. While keeping the old faithful French
and British families of the past the congregation has developed on a huge scale. The new migrants have brought
in a great deal of valuable expertise and fresh talent. Anne
Dobinson has been organist for a number of years and Tony
and Carole Rogers have contributed their expertise and
knowledge in care of the sacristy and serving at the altar.
Doreen Collier the treasurer confidently handles finances

Miss Elizabeth Hannay MBE at an audience with Pope John Paul in recognition of her services to ecumenism centred on St Bartholomew's Church. She is wearing the uniform of a major in the US Army in which she served as an intelligence officer during the Second World War.

in French, English and United States currency, while Diana Wilson with her skill in flower arranging and Irene Bishop as manager of the household arrangements of the chaplain's flat lead a team which ensures the property is maintained in good order. Eric Lambert, John and Monica Lewis and others have greatly reduced the cost of repairs with their ready help and practical expertise. Lately Brian Cordery who worked as a solicitor in Paris where he was churchwarden of St Michael's has become honorary secretary of the Association at a time when legal knowledge has been vital. Most encouraging is a licensed pastoral assistant and prospective ordinand, only the second in the history of the church, John Gay who is embarking on the long and arduous training for ordination. Our long-standing visiting chaplain and Cure

The interior of St Bartholomew's with the British Ambassador and
Julian Thompson before the visit of HRH Prince Edward and the
Countess of Wessex.

of Souls before his retirement in 2000, Donald Pankhurst
has remarked that St Bartholomew's is becoming more and
more like a thriving English parish.

The church itself has never looked better. The organ has
been completely restored and renovated in 2002 and the
library is at long last free of damp. The pulpit is no longer
a hazardous place to stand as it was for at least thirty years
and every part of the building has been lovingly cared for.
Also as a witness and tribute to the members of St Bartholomew's, a new and very striking stained glass window has
been placed in the last plain glass light beside the 'Avranches windows' on the north wall. Designed, measured and
constructed by the Pierpont family, it was dedicated by
Bishop Frank Sargeant, former Bishop at Lambeth and now
an assistant bishop in the Diocese in Europe at the St
Bartholomew's Day Eucharist in 2001. Everything is in order
for the Third Millennium.

The Right Reverend Frank Sargeant with the Reverend Alan Charters after the dedication of the St Bartholomew window, 24 August 2001.

Of the questions which remain, one remains outstanding for the future of St Bartholomew's. Unlike the past generations of English-speaking Dinardais, will this new generation of incomers produce children who will want to remain and make their own futures in Brittany; or will they, like their predecessors return to their native land to pursue their education and careers? With the increasing development of the European Union it has never been easier to settle and work in other parts of Europe and so far, the Breton people have been most welcoming to the British incomers. The economy benefits from their presence and they have helped to keep the declining countryside alive by buying up and restoring old and dilapidated property. The prospects for a permanent English settlement have never been better.

But for the first time in its history St Bartholomew's is not dependent solely on the immigrants and visitors from English-speaking communities. Amongst the congregation there is now a considerable number of French and other worshippers who find Anglican worship the appropriate way

The exterior of St Bartholomew's Church, 1980.

to converse with God. They bring to the church a new sense of a wider community and an enlarged understanding of the universal Church.

So our story ends, a story of successive communities who have loved their church and independently ensured its continuance, communities who have nevertheless been loyal to the Anglican traditions which first inspired the building of the church, communities who have been inspired to open the doors to all who wished to worship with them regardless of denomination, creed or race. At one Easter in recent times there were people from twenty-six nations present including the last remaining members of the Romanov family, the Royal Family of Russia, and more recently, the Earl and Countess of Wessex attended the Eucharist.

With these and other recollections of the past goes responsibility for the future. St Bartholomew's is the last remaining Anglican church in Brittany, although a new congregation without a permanent building has been developed in the south of Brittany in an attempt to widen the opportunities to meet the needs of the recent English-speaking incomers. With 35,000 people British people living in Brittany there is an immense work to be done to make the church known and available, for the lonely and the sick and for those who need spiritual sustenance. The work of the Church throughout the world, founded as it is on the inspiration and knowledge of Jesus Christ, continues through all the changes and chances, meeting new challenges, often facing indifference and accusations of irrelevance. Yet throughout the ages, as a result of the faith and conviction of very ordinary people, it quietly goes on answering the needs of the people around, many of whom did not realise they had that need until the crisis came and they needed the friendship and love of an unthreatening yet practical community.

The Organ in
St Bartholomew's Church

The instrument was built in 1894 by Moley Young Alfred Oldknow
Organ builders, orginally in London who moved to Jersey and built a
number of organs in Brittany including the great organ in the
principal church in Dinan. The Chaplain and organist of St
Bartholomew's were impressed by the quality of this organ and
recommended that the committee should invite Alfred Oldknow to
build the organ in the church (see Chapter 4).

Since its construction it has been overhauled regularly:

1922 by F. Clauss et Fils of Rennes
1928 by James Ivines of Southampton
1967 by Beuchet-Deberre of Nantes
In 1971 by Y. Severe of Le Mans
1975 by A. Mack of Dinan
1990 by Ian Fox of The King's School, Gloucester
2001 by Gildas Menoret of Nantes

Composition of the Instrument

First keyboard. Grand Orgue. 56 notes:

1. Bourdon 8'   4. Doublette 2'
2. Open Diapason 8'   5. Nasard 2 2/3
3. Clarabella 8'   6. Tierce 1 3/5
4. Prestant 4'

Second keyboard. Recit expressif. 56 notes:

7. Lieblich Gedackt 8   10. Fourniture IIIIrgs
8. Diapason 8'   11. Trumpte 8'
9. Principal 4'

Pedalboard of 30 notes:

12. Bourdon 16'

Accessories: Tremolo
                 Tirasse I
                 Tirasse II
                 Copulae II/I

Chaplains at
St Bartholomew's Dinard

22nd December 1873	The Reverend Anthony Francis Thomson
19th October 1877	The Reverend Arthur Keville Davies Edwards
30th April 1890	The Reverend Richard Peck
1st October 1895	The Reverend Percy Carmichael Clarke
29th November 1904	The Reverend Frederick Edmeston Freese
11th February 1907	The Reverend Cyril John Valpy French
10th January 1908	The Reverend Herbert Fleming Bergin Townsend Mills
January 1923	The Reverend J.C. Vallance
October 1930	The Reverend G.C.Morrow
May 1934	The Reverend Walter Green.
June 1936	The Reverend F. Gwynne Davies.
July 1939	The Reverend C.H.D.Grimes
14th January 1940	The Reverend Hugh Jones
10th May 1940	Colonel Karl Cate (not officially licensed by the Bishop)

After the Second World War, there was no permanent chaplain and the church opened only during Easter and the summer months. A very large number of clergy from Britain and elsewhere overseas came to do duty. Their names, followed by the first date on which they came with the number of visits they have made are recorded below.

Ackworth, A.J.P.	1997(2)	Bicknell, N.L.	1953(1)
Allen, Michael	1995(3)	Billet, Anthony	1993(1)
		Birdwell, M.L.	1952(1)
Baker, Albert	1999(1)	Birney, James	1978(2)USA
Bard, Christopher	1988(1)	Blows, Derek	. 1993(1)
Betts, George	1966(1)	Boyes, Charles	1961(1)

Briggs, H.C.J.	1955(2)	Goss, Thomas A.	1971(1)Jersey
Brown, Rt. Rev. Thomas		Greensides, Leonard	1965(10)
	1996(4)NZ	Grieve, A.C.	1996(1)
Brownrigg, C.A.G.	1948 (13)	Griffiths, D.N.	1968(1)
Budd, J.V.	1965(1)	Grimes, C.N.D.	1951(1)
Butler, M.J.	1964(1)		
		Hall, Geoffrey	1960(1)
Casey, R.M.	1955(1)	Halliwell, Michael	1999(1)Jersey
Cate, Karl	1946(2)	Hamilton, Michael	2001(1)USA
Charters, Alan	1966(21)*	Handley, Ven. Michael	1986(1)
Cherry, Malcolm	1995(1)	Hasleden, E.J.C.	1958(1)
Churchill, Very Rev. J.	1990(1)	Hawkins, Allen N.G.	1959(1)
Cogman, Very Rev. F.		Haynes, Peter N.S.	1970(3)
	1957(4)Guernsey	Hickman, J.S.	1968(1)
Collard, F.W.	1957(1)	Hill, A.S.	1974(1)USA
Colman, J.B.	1962(1)	Hogg, W.B.	1959(1)
Conway, Alfred	1982(5)	Hyde, V.D.W.	1970(1)
Corrigan, Rt. Rev. Daniel			
	1966(1)USA	Illing, Eric	2000(1)
Cripps, Michael	1997(1)		
Curtis, Geoffrey C.R.	1947(17)*	James, David E.	1966(1)
		Jay, R.	1999(2)
Davis, G.M.	1950(1)	Jennings, Eric H.	1967(1)
Dawson-Walker, F.	1945(3)	Johns, Donald	1974(1)
Denes, Charles	1982(1)	Jones, David I.S.	1970(1)
Derwent, Rt. Rev. Frederick			
	1995(1)Scot	Kelley, A.D.	1958(1)
Diaper, Trevor	1993(1)	Kenraugh, Thomas	1991(1)
Dooley, B.	1981(2)USA	Kingston, P.D.	1966(1)
Dunbar, J.W.	1949(1)	Kingston, William S.	1967(1)
Dunbar, L.	1968(1)		
Dupleux, L.	1964(1)	Landreth, D.	1970(1)
		Larsen, Gilbert S.	1989(1)USA
Evans, Ven.Barrie	1997(1)Wales	Leah, Andrew	1980(1)
Evans, Ven.Kenneth	1968(1)	Leo, Very Rev. James R.	
Eyre, Richard M.S.	1967(1)		1984(3)Paris
		Littlechild, William	1957(1)
Finlay, Terence	1967(2)USA,Can	Loughbotough, G.W.	1971(1)
		Lyons, P.B.	1984(1)
Gibson, R.M.	1956(6)		
Gilbert, Roger	1973(13)	Maples, Jeffrey S.	1989(1)
Gillhespey, Charles	1994(2)	Marshall, Bryan	1998(1)
Godfrey, M.B.S.	1965(1)	Marvell, John	1997(4)
Good, R.S.	1967(1)	Massey, R.	1955(1)
Goodrich, Brian	1972(1)	Menzies, A.C.V.	1965(1)

Miller, David	1968(1)	Shelford, G.H.R.N.	1987(1)
Morgan, Christopher	1983(1)	Shell, Charles	1969(1)
Morgan, Philip	1997(2)	Simpson, John Arthur	1971(1)
Morris, John	1980(3)	Stephens, P.R.	1976(1)
		Stevenson, Keith	1976(1)
Newell, N.W.	1951(1)	Streeting, J. Laurence	1959(5)
Newman, L.	1994(2)		
Noble, C.W.A.	1961(1)NI	Taylor, T.R.B.	1986(2)NI
Nye, C.S.	1968(3)	Thomas, E. Manley	1955(1)
		Thursfield, G.M.R.	1952(1)
Pankhurst, Donald	1972(25)*	Topham, Paul	1987(1)
Pennant, Philip	1991(2)	Tyndall, Timothy	1992(1)
Perry, Christopher	1978(1)		
Pollard, Geoffrey	1969(2)	Vaughan, R. John	1965(1)
Poston, Robert	1981(1)	Vidler, Very Rev. Alec R	1956(1)
Poulain, Pasteur Andre			
	1946(1)France	Waller, Ven. David J.	
			1985(1)Canada
Randall, Gareth	1995(6)	Ward, R. Somerset	1948(1)
Robinson, Rt. Rev. Harold		Westmore, W.H.	1948(7)
	1978(1)USA	Whitmore, Robert	1970(1)USA
Rose, David	1958(1)	Whitehead, Arthur	1967(1)
Rounds, P.R.	1976(1)	Wigley, H.M.	1974(1)
Rowlands, E.	1976(6)	Williams, David	1982(1)
Russell, A.S.	1962(2)	Williams, John	1979(2)
		Williams, T.H.	1965(1)
Sabowier, Robert	1958(1)	Wilmot, Philip	1993(1)
Schaeffer, John	2000(3)USA	Wilmot, Laurence F.	1966(1)
Schiff, Leonard	1960(4)	Wilson, Arthur	1998(1)
Semple, Michael	1959(1)	Wilson, W. John	1990(2)
Senor, H.	1981(1)	Wolfe, K.W.	1963(1)
Sergeant, Rt Rev. Frank	1986(5)	Wright, Rt. Rev. Clifford	
Sexton, J.L.	1953(1)		1997(3)Wales
Shaw, Frederick	1980(1)		

All locum chaplains mentioned above come from the Church of
England except where otherwise noted. All have come to take duty at
their own expense on a 'house for duty' basis.

Index